THE THEOLOGY OF THE SECOND CHAIR:

A Theological Foundation for the Subordinate Leader

of the Local Church

ISBN: 978-0-557-46331-2

For my children,

Brady Jack, Cooper Gray, & Carson Claire:

You are my greatest delight!

TABLE OF CONTENTS

INTRODUCTION

In his timeless work, *Spiritual Leadership*, J. Oswald Sanders states, "'Full of

wisdom' was one of the requirements for even subordinate leaders in the early church (Acts

6:3)."[1] This statement by Sanders highlights a great need for the development of

subordinate leaders, both of the early church, and of the church today. Kevin Lawson,

author of *How to Thrive in Associate Staff Ministry* writes:

> In North America, the number of churches with associate staff members and
> churches with more than one associate staff member is growing. . . . These associate
> staff people serve their churches in a variety of ways. . . . Some are involved in pastoral
> care and counseling, and others focus on administration. Still others find themselves
> wearing multiple hats, carrying more than one kind of responsibility. Historically,
> associate staff positions can be traced to "apprenticeship" arrangements in which the
> "minister in training" learned the ministry by assisting an experienced church pastor in
> his duties. With the exception of some music staff positions, the development of
> permanent associate staff positions is primarily a 20th century phenomenon. It had its
> beginnings in the late 19th century with the growth of church religious education
> programs.[2]

As the church has grown and expanded in the last century, there has developed a

growing need for both staff specialists and generalists to assist, serve, and lead in different

facets of the congregation. Thus, Lawson concludes, "The growth of this ministry field has

been accompanied by a variety of stresses and problems. In general, associate staff positions

have been characterized by relatively brief tenures and high attrition rates."[3] This fact is

---

[1] J. Oswald Sanders, *Spiritual Leadership: Principles of Excellence for Every Believer* (Chicago: Moody Press, 1994), 57-8.

[2] Kevin Lawson, *How to Thrive in Associate Staff Ministry* (Herndon, VA: The Alban Institute, 2000), 3.

[3] Ibid., 4.

unfortunate, unnecessary and with focused training, the effects of it can be lessened.

In recent years, much has been made of the need for excellent leadership in the local church, and thus there has been a vast increase in the development of leadership resources available to church leaders. These much needed resources have provided great insight to leaders in the church on what it is to lead effectively in God's kingdom. Furthermore, pastors and staff members alike all across North America flock to conferences on the subject matter of leadership in the church. Yet, despite this, very little has been written directly to the associate staff member as both a leader and a follower. The reality is that the majority of leadership messages to the local church are written for and spoken to the lead leader, the senior pastor. This has the tendency to produce frustration in the lives of the subordinate leaders who are often quite capable, but in the area of leadership development are poorly resourced. This has been the case in this author's life because most if not all of the resources he was reading were written to someone else, in a different role, experiencing a different reality on a daily basis.

This led this author and his colleague, Mike Bonem, to study and discuss together what it truly is to be a leader in the church as an associate staff member. The result of this discussion led to the development of a resource, *Leading from the Second Chair: Serving Your Church, Fulfilling Your Role, and Realizing Your Dreams*. To what we call "second chair leaders," Mike and I write:

We want you to understand that you are not alone. God desires to use this experience in the second chair as a transforming season in your life. As you read this book, we hope you become aware that God has a specific role for you to play and incredible potential for you to realize. This role will challenge your ego, buffer your speech, and keep you anchored in your calling. It is a place of growth and development, a place of real contribution, and a place that tests your commitment. God wants your best wherever you are, no matter the circumstances, no matter the comfort level of your chair. To put it bluntly, the chair in which you sit is not a "La-z-boy"! It is often the most uncomfortable chair in the room, but it can be deeply fulfilling.[4]

Definition of Terms

There are a number of terms that need to be defined for the reader to understand this topic. The first term, "second chair leader," includes anyone in a subordinate role, whose influence with others adds value throughout the organization.[5] The term, subordinate, will be examined thoroughly through the thesis, thus, it is important to define what it is to be subordinate. We state, "Even the most gifted or capable second chair is still under the leadership and authority of another leader."[6] Thus, to be a subordinate, is to be one under the leadership and authority of another. This has the potential to include any associate staff member, not just an associate pastor or executive pastor. This could also include lay leaders who impact the organization in a substantial way. For this study though, the term second chair leader will be used for associate staff members. The second term is "lead leader," also called, "first chair leader." These terms are used to describe the senior pastor of the local church.

---

[4] Mike Bonem and Roger Patterson, *Leading from the Second Chair: Serving Your Church, Fulfilling Your Role, and Realizing Your Dreams* (San Francisco: Jossey-Bass, 2005), 2.

[5] Ibid.

In *Leading from the Second Chair* we sought to provide a framework for second chair leadership. This framework is described as the three apparent paradoxes of second chair leadership. This also is terminology of great importance. We wrote:

> It is these challenges that we refer to as the apparent paradoxes of second chair leadership. We label them as subordinate-leader, deep-wide, and contentment-dreaming. They are paradoxes because at first glance they seem to be mutually exclusive. But our contention is that these pairs do not represent 'either/or' choices. Rather, effective second chair leaders need to live within each of these paradoxes and master both ends of the spectrum. Some may experience the tension of one paradox more intensely than another, but all three paradoxes are woven into the fabric of being a second chair leader.[7]

The paradoxes deal with the relational aspect of being an associate staff member (subordinate-leader), the daily discipline of serving the local church (deep-wide), and the deeply felt dreams that are within the heart of the second chair leader (contentment-dreaming).

To validate our framework, we set out to interview 17 associate staff members all over the country. At nearly every turn, these interviewees affirmed the apparent paradoxes as a frequent reality. Not only did these interviews serve to validate the framework of the three paradoxes, but they also surfaced the interviewee's excitement about a leadership resource geared directly to their ministry setting as they, too, had experienced a dearth of material in this area. In the foreword to the work, Greg Hawkins of Willow Creek Community Church expands on this idea as he states:

---

[6] Ibid., 14.

[7] Mike Bonem and Roger Patterson, "Three Paradoxes for Every Second Chair Leader," *The Pastor's Coach: Equipping the Leaders of Today's Church*, by Dan Reiland, Vol. 6, no. 16 (August): 2. (Article published in bi-monthly newsletter, www.injoy.com.)

Over the years I have regularly gotten calls and emails from executive pastors asking for my advice on how to be more effective in their role. They have asked me what books I have read or seminars I have attended that have helped me over the years. And I come up empty every time. I don't know of anything that addresses the complexities and tensions that are unique to the second chair role. . . . That is why it is so exciting for me to introduce you to Mike, Roger and *Leading from the Second Chair*.

Drawing on their years of second chair experience, as well as the experience of other skilled second chair leaders, Mike and Roger have captured the essence of the second chair role. It is about leading and managing your way through a set of paradoxes. The first time Mike shared the three key paradoxes with me, I immediately knew that they were on to something. It rang so true to my experience.

I remember the day I figured out that Bill Hybels wanted me to boldly lead like a first chair leader, not just "manage" the church staff. Yet I had to do that knowing that he could step in at any time and reverse the decision I had just made. This was counter-intuitive to everything I had ever read about leadership (Paradox of Subordinate-Leader).

As executive pastor I am expected to know something about everything going on at Willow Creek, and at the same time to provide hands on leadership of a multi-million dollar capital campaign, while providing world-class coaching to the high school pastor and a dozen other ministry leaders. The pressure associated with that is immense (Paradox of Deep-Wide).

And finally, there have been days when I have dreamed intensely about the future of my church. Dreams so real that I am sure that God would want them to come alive right away. And yet ultimately my dreams are just one voice in a larger community, under someone else's leadership. I have had to learn to trust God and wait on him patiently (Paradox of Contentment-Dreaming).[8]

Hawkins' insights into the second chair role affirm the work of *Leading from the Second Chair* and lend validity to their framework for second chair leadership. Yet, we only touched on the theology for second chair leadership in *Leading from the Second Chair*. Instead of utilizing an array of examples and establishing the numerous expressions of this type of leadership in the Scripture, we tried to weave the story of Joseph through the text.

---

[8] Bonem and Patterson, *Leading From the Second Chair,* ix-x.

What you have in your hands will go beyond the three apparent paradoxes of second chair leadership as found in *Leading from the Second Chair*, and examine a variety of roles and relationships found throughout the Scripture to establish the theological foundation. The theological foundation will begin with the investigation of the doctrine of the Trinity to examine the authority structure within the Trinity. There will also be an examination of a number of passages of Scripture that establish the formal relationship of various Old and New Testament subordinate leaders to their lead leaders. The author will then examine the various roles and character traits of these subordinate leaders in the section entitled Applying Theology in the Second Chair. This section will be developed for application of these lessons so that they might be applied to the local church setting.

THE THEOLOGICAL FOUNDATION OF THE SECOND CHAIR

In the economy of Scripture there are guidelines for effectively serving and leading while under the authority of another. These guidelines and principles have at their foundation an understanding that God is the source of ultimate authority. Being the source of authority, God then grants authority to various leaders to accomplish His purpose. God often then provides these leaders with subordinates who are to serve under their authority and who are to lead out in various capacities to fulfill God's purpose. This provision of leaders who serve with an attitude of subordination and lead within the authority that they have been granted is modeled in the Trinity and can be seen in various forms throughout the Scripture. Both the Trinity and a variety of examples from both the Old and New Testaments will establish this theological foundation.

The Trinity

Subordinate leadership has as its origin the relationships expressed in the Trinity in which God the Son and God the Holy Spirit are subject to the supreme authority of God the Father in their administrative role in the Godhead. [9] Concerning the ontology of the Godhead, Charles Ryrie states, "Generation and procession occur within the divine Being

---

[9] Bruce A.Ware, *Father, Son, and Holy Spirit: Roles, Relationships, & Relevance* (Wheaton, IL: Crossway Books, 2005), 66.

and carry with them no thought of subordination of essence."[10] The Father, Son, and Spirit

have always been co-eternal. Yet, administratively, there is a clear demonstration of

procession and the granting of authority within the Godhead. Bruce Ware states, "Rightful

places of authority are respected in Scripture, and the greatest example of this is God the

Father."[11] Jesus made this clear in John 5:19 when He said, "The Son can do nothing by

himself; he can do only what he sees his Father doing, because whatever the Father does the

Son also does."[12]

It is important to make the distinction concerning the functional roles of the persons

of the Godhead in order to avoid appearing to advocate Subordinationism. This doctrine

taught that ". . . the Son and the Spirit were subordinate to God; created by God, albeit

before all worlds, but nevertheless created. Jesus Christ was a man adopted by God and

raised to the rank of divinity rather than co-eternal Son of God coming down from heaven

and taking our nature upon Him."[13] This anti-trinitarian view was made known by Arius

(ca. 250-336), who taught that the Son was generated by the Father, and that the Spirit was

the first of the Son's creations, since all things were made by Him.[14]

To be exact, for the purposes of this theological foundation the idea of

---

[10] Charles C. Ryrie, *Basic Theology: A Popular Systematic Guide to Understanding Biblical Truth* (Colorado Springs: Victor Books, 1999), 54.

[11] Ware, *Father, Son, and Holy Spirit,* 65-6.

[12] John 5:19, *NIV.*

[13] J. S. Whale, *Christian Doctrine* (Cambridge: University Press, 1941), 116.

[14] Ryrie, *Basic Theology,* 56.

subordination and granting of authority found in the Godhead pertain only to the administrative relationship of the Godhead. Wayne Grudem terms this administrative distinction as "economic subordination" in which the Son and Spirit are "equal in being but subordinate in role."[15] This idea is central to the doctrine of the Trinity and was first affirmed in the Nicene Creed.[16] Ware states of the relationship of the Father and Son, "The Son in fact is the eternal Son of the eternal Father, and hence, the Son stands in relationship of eternal submission under the authority of His Father."[17]

Jesus' Claims of Subordination and Authority

Being the source of all authority, God the Father granted all authority to the Son to accomplish through His atonement and establishment of the church the redemptive purposes of the Father.[18] Having received this authority from the Father, Jesus fulfilled the task that the Father sent Him to accomplish. A treatment of two significant Greek terms, both meaning "to send," will assist the reader in understanding how Jesus' earthly ministry was filled with claims of both subordination and authority. The terms are *pempo* and *apostello*.

The first term, *pempo,* carries a meaning of being sent temporarily as if on an errand or specific mission.[19] Jesus used this term 30 times, denoting of Himself that His

---

[15] Wayne Grudem, *Systematic Theology: An Introduction to Biblical Doctrine* (Leicester: Inter-Varsity Press and Zondervan, 1994), 251.

[16] Ibid.

[17] Ware, *Father, Son, and Holy Spirit,* 71.

[18] See John 17:2; Matt 28:18; Eph 1:22.

[19] Strong, *Strong's Exhaustive Concordance,* 56.

work was, "to do the will of him who sent me and to finish his work."[20] Hubert Ritt states,

"Of the 79 occurrences of this verb in the New Testament, the 32 in John (24 of those

referring to the sending of Jesus) are noteworthy, as are the 21 in Luke-Acts. While

apostello occurs 42 times in Mark and Matthew together, *pempo* occurs in Mark and

Matthew only five times."[21]

The second term, *apostello*, also means to send out on a mission,[22] send forth, or

send out.[23] Jan-Adolf Buhner states, "When it is not used to circumscribe the successful

completion of a messenger's journey . . . but is sharpened to focus on the purpose and goal

of the event in question and hence on the sending forth and completion of the assignment,

the verb assumes the meaning of commission."[24] This commission assumes authority from

the one who is sending the messenger. Buhner further states, "Objects of *apostello* are,

correspondingly, persons of whom the sender can expect obedience and the willingness to

serve as messengers (workers in Matt 20:2; servants in Mark 12:2-5; helpers in Acts 19:22;

disciples in Matt 22:16; Mark 11:1; 14:13; Luke 7:18, 20; the son in Mark 12:6)."[25]

The Apostle John makes use of both terms in a substantial way in his gospel.

---

[20] John 4:34, *NIV*.

[21] Horst Balz and Gerhard Schneider, eds., *Exegetical Dictionary of the New Testament*, vol. 3, "Pempo," by Hubert Ritt (Grand Rapids: Wm. B. Eerdmans Publishing, 1993), 68.

[22] Strong, *Strong's Exhaustive Concordance*, 15.

[23] Horst Balz and Gerhard Schneider, eds., *Exegetical Dictionary of the New Testament*, vol. 1, "Apostello," by Jan-Adolf Buhner (Grand Rapids: Wm. B. Eerdmans Publishing, 1990), 141.

[24] Ibid., 141-2.

[25] Ibid., 142.

Apostello is used 28 times in John and is used primarily to communicate Christology

through its 19 uses in relation to Jesus.[26] Buhner states:

> Under the influence of Jewish teaching about sending, John develops this tradition (1
> John 4:9, 10, 14; John 3:16f.) into the basis for Christological legitimation (5:36, 38;
> 6:29, 57; 7:29; 10:36; 11:42; 17:3, 8, 18): *apostello* denotes commissioning and
> authorization from God. The sending discloses the unique manner in which the Son is
> bound to the Father; a believing acknowledgement of the phrase "that you have sent
> me" therefore constitutes the goal and content of confession (11:42; 17:3, 8, 21, 23,
> 25).[27]

For Jesus to be sent by the Father then is to be commissioned by God and authorized by God

to accomplish the specific task of completing the redemptive work of God. Thus, Jesus is

subordinate because the Father can send Him, yet Jesus is also in authority as He is sent to

accomplish a great mission. Jesus then commissions those who follow Him by saying,

"Peace be with you! As the Father has sent me, I am sending you."[28]

The Apostle John also makes special use of *pempo* in his gospel. Ritt states, "In

John the actual historical sending of the Son by the Father is expressed in Jesus' own words

in the formula *o pemphas me* (4:34, 5:24, 30, 37; 6:38, 39, 44; 7:16, 28, 33; 8:16, 18, 26, 29;

9:4; 12:44, 45, 49; 13:20; 14:24; 15:21; 16:5). These 22 occurrences, along with statements

in the third person referring to the Father or God 'who sent him' (5:23; 7:18), reveal the

christological theocentricity of the Father-Son relationship."[29] Clearly, from Jesus' own

---

[26] Ibid., 141.

[27] Ibid., 142.

[28] John 20:21, *NIV.*

[29] Balz and Schneider, eds., *Exegetical Dictionary of the New Testament*, vol. 3, "Pempo," by
Hubert Ritt, 68.

words and from the gospel writer's recording of these words, there is no doubt that the sending of the Son was initiated by the Father. This sending later flowed down from Jesus to His disciples, and, as Ritt states, "The continuation of this sending by Jesus involves the believing disciples . . . the Jewish principle that the messenger bears the same authority as the one who sent him comes into play."[30] Thus within the usage of both of these terms, there is a clear picture of Jesus' subordination to the Father, His being granted authority to accomplish the Father's mission, and further granting of authority to His subordinates.

The Son and the Spirit

Jesus gave the gift of the Holy Spirit, the gifts of grace to the individual members of the church body[31] and also appointed officers to the church so that those in His body might be governed and equipped for the works of service and the building of His body.[32] This is all to be accomplished through the leading and empowering of the indwelling Holy Spirit.

It must be noted that Jesus and the Holy Spirit practice mutual submission to one another in order to complete the task that the Father gave to Jesus. Clearly, Jesus accomplished all that He accomplished by following the Holy Spirit,[33] being full of the Holy

---

[30] Ibid.

[31] See Eph 4:7; Rom 12:6-8; 1 Cor 12:4-11.

[32] See Eph 4:11-12; Acts 14:23; 20:17; Titus 1:5; 1 Pet 5:1-2.

[33] See Isa 11:1-2 and Ware, *Father, Son, and Holy Spirit,* 88.

Spirit and being led by the Spirit.[34] William Evans states, "How dependent Jesus Christ was, in His state of humiliation, on the Holy Spirit! If He needed to depend solely upon the Spirit, can we afford to do less?"[35] In summation, Evans says of Jesus that He was conceived by and born of the Spirit (Luke 1:35); led by the Spirit (Matt 4:1); anointed by the Spirit for service (Acts 10:38); crucified in the power of the Spirit (Heb 9:14); raised by the power of the Spirit (Rom 1:4, 8:11).[36]

Yet, the Spirit was also subordinate to the Son. The doctrine of double procession teaches that the Spirit proceeded both from the Father and the Son. This comes from John 15:26 which states, "When the Counselor comes, whom I will send to you from the Father, the Spirit of truth who goes out from the Father, he will testify about me."[37]

Two further examples from John's gospel are John 16:7 and John 16:13-15 which state:

> But I tell you the truth: It is for your good that I am going away. Unless I go away, the Counselor will not come to you; but if I go, I will send him to you.[38] But when he, the Spirit of truth, comes, he will guide you into all truth. He will not speak on his own; he will speak only what he hears, and he will tell you what is yet to come. He will bring glory to me by taking from what is mine and making it known to you. All that belongs to the Father is mine. That is why I said the Spirit will take from what is mine and make it known to you.[39]

---

[34] Luke 4:1-2.

[35] William Evans, *The Great Doctrines of the Bible* (Chicago: Moody Press, 1980), 119.

[36] Ibid.

[37] John 15:26, *NIV*.

[38] John 16:7, *NIV*.

[39] John 16:13-15, *NIV*.

Of John 16:13-15, Brooke Westcott states, "The verb is left absolute. The fact which is

declared is that the teaching of the Spirit comes finally from the one source of Truth. The

words that follow show that no distinction is made in this respect between that which is of

the Father and that which is of Christ."[40] Thus, there is no distinction to be made of whether

or not the Spirit is only of the Son or only of the Father, but is of both the Son and Father.

H. A. Ironside states:

> He was going away, and another Person of the Godhead was now to be sent to the earth
> who was not to become incarnate in one Person, but who was to work through the
> whole Church, empowering the servants of God as they proclaimed His message. . . .
> Notice, that during the Old Testament dispensation we have God the Father working.
> God the Son was working directly in the days of His flesh. Now, since Christ has
> returned to the right hand of God, and has taken His place as Mediator, the Father and
> the Son have sent another Person of the Godhead, and He is here working in this world,
> and will remain here carrying on this glorious work until the consummation of this age.
> Notice, incidentally, how the Deity of our Lord Jesus Christ is implied in these words.
> Can you think of any man, no matter how good, no matter how godly, no matter how
> powerful, daring to say of the blessed Holy Spirit, "I will send Him?" Why, we see the
> very opposite in Scripture. The Holy Ghost sends men out into the world, men do not
> send Him. But Jesus was more than man, He was God and Man in One adorable,
> wonderful Person, and therefore He could say with confidence, "I will send the
> Comforter, the Paraclete, to bear witness, when I have gone back to the glory."[41]

Historically, these passages and this issue of the Spirit proceeding from the Son and

Father were at the heart of a split between the eastern (Orthodox) Christianity and western

(Roman Catholic) Christianity. The controversy stemmed from a revision of the Nicene

---

[40] Brooke Foss Westcott, *The Gospel According to St. John: The Greek Text with Introduction and Notes*, ed. A. Westcott (Grand Rapids: Baker Book House, 1980), 224.

[41] H.A. Ironside, *Addresses on the Gospel of John* (Neptune, New York: Loizeaux Brothers, Inc, 1942), 690-1. It is not this author's intent to discuss the ages or dispensations in this thesis. The intent of this quote is to demonstrate how the work of the Holy Spirit would further the Kingdom message after Jesus' ascension and also how Ironside affirms the deity of Jesus and the subordination of the Spirit to Jesus.

Creed, where in A.D. 589, the term *filoque,* Latin for "and from the Son," was inserted to state that the Spirit proceeds from the Father and the Son.[42] The controversy that followed was based on the understanding that this phrase taught that the Holy Spirit was eternally from the Son, versus at a point in time, namely Pentecost.[43] It appears that the Spirit is to be sent by Jesus, bring glory to Jesus, and work in accordance with Jesus and the Father to make known the plan of reconciliation, and this is done so at a point in history. Grudem states, "And if the Son together with the Father sends the Spirit into the world, by analogy it would seem appropriate to say that this reflects eternal ordering of their relationships."[44]

The Trinity, Authority and Subordination

What should one conclude about the nature and characteristics of the Trinity at this point? First, God the Father is the source of ultimate authority and Jesus and the Holy Spirit, the source of subordination. Or, more forcefully, to be God the Father is to be in authority and share authority. To be God the Son or God the Spirit is to be in subordination to the Father and mutually to one another. Ware goes so far as to say, "It is the nature of God both to exert authority and to obey in submission. And since this is the eternal nature of God, we may know that it is beautiful and it is good."[45]

Second, the persons of the Trinity grant authority to completely fulfill the

---

[42] Grudem, *Systematic Theology*, 246.

[43] Ibid.

[44] Ibid., 247.

[45] Ware, *Father, Son, and Holy Spirit, 85.*

redemptive mission of God. This takes place as God the Father grants all authority to Jesus. Jesus then grants authority to the Spirit to lead, empower, and accomplish the task of redemption that is to be accomplished through the church.

Third, the Trinitarian model of authority, subordination, the granting of authority, and mutual subordination has important implications for lead leaders and subordinate leaders in the local church. These principles are modeled by the Godhead and should be understood and applied to the relationships of authority and subordination in believers' lives. More succinctly, for the purposes of this thesis, these principles should be understood and applied by the subordinate leaders of the local church, and the application of these principles will be developed in the section focusing on application.

Subordinate Leaders from the Old Testament

This section will examine the Old Testament passages that express the subordinate relationship of Aaron, Joshua, and the Judges appointed by Moses to govern. It will also examine the subordinate relationship of Elisha to Elijah when Elisha served as Elijah's attendant.

Aaron's Subordination to Moses

There are a substantial number of Old Testament examples of subordinate leaders who served under the authority of a great leader. Moses is one of the most obvious examples of a leader who was surrounded by capable subordinate leaders. Throughout his leadership of the people of Israel, Moses learned to be a leader who granted his subordinates authority to perform the tasks of leading while they followed his leadership. The first

example from leaders who served under Moses is that of Aaron. While Moses, at his initial

calling, was arguing with Yahweh about his inability to confront Pharoah and lead the

Israelites out of Egypt, Yahweh mercifully spoke these words of provision to him. The

Scripture states:

> Then the LORD's anger burned against Moses and he said, "What about your brother, Aaron the Levite? I know he can speak well. He is already on his way to meet you, and his heart will be glad when he sees you. You shall speak to him and put words in his mouth; I will help both of you speak and will teach you what to do. He will speak to the people for you, and it will be as if he were your mouth and as if you were God to him."[46]

In this situation Aaron was to play the role of spokesman for Moses. Moses was declaring

his inadequacy as a public speaker. Yahweh decided to make provision for Moses by

providing for him another leader to assist him where he had need. Further, as Yahweh is

calling Moses to go, He places Aaron under Moses' authority so that it is clear that Moses is

to "put words in his mouth," and, "it will be as if he were your mouth and as if you were

God to him." C.F. Keil and F. Delitszch state, "Aaron would stand in the same relation to

Moses, as a prophet to God: the prophet only spoke what God inspired him with, and Moses

should be the inspiring God to him."[47]

Very few commentators make much of Aaron and his role of spokesman. The

commentaries, instead, deal with Moses' weakness, his lack of faith, and his comfort when

---

[46] Exod 4:14-16, *NIV.*

[47] C. F. Keil and F. Delitzsch, *The Pentateuch: Three Volumes in One* in vol. 1 of *Commentary on the Old Testament* (Peabody, MA: Hendrickson Publishers, 1989), 451.

Yahweh provides another to go with him. Arthur Pink states, "We are more ready to trust anything than the living God. We move along with bold decision when we possess the countenance and support of a poor frail mortal like ourselves, but we falter, hesitate, and demur when we have the light of the master's countenance to cheer us, and the strength of His omnipotent arm to support us."[48]

Another line of thought concerning the Aaron provision in this text is that it is a later redaction to this passage where a pro-Aaron insertion became important to his legacy. John I. Durham states:

> A theory generally accepted in most of this research concerning Aaron is that a wide recognition of Aaron as the priest *par excellence* came late in OT history, certainly after the Exile, bur far enough ahead of the final formation of the books of the tetrateuch to permit the insertion of pro-Aaron material at selected appropriate points. The section at hand presents such a point though one at which the role of Aaron is promoted not exclusively, but in association with and clearly secondary to that of Moses.[49]

J. A. Motyer takes exception to Durham's assertion of general acceptance that a redactor inserted a pro-Aaron section into this narrative. Motyer contends that Yahweh is being merciful in providing Aaron to Moses, and he disagrees, stating, "I find myself baffled how anyone could find the reference to Aaron 'confusing the sequence…a kind of postscript' as Durham claims to do. The verses read smoothly and fit in a natural

---

[48] Arthur W. Pink, *Gleanings in Exodus* (Chicago: Moody Press, 1977), 39. It is interesting to note that the truthful story of Moses' response to Yahweh is a mirror reflecting every man's lack of faith, as Pink instructs. But Pink runs right past the beautiful solution that Yahweh brings to Moses in sending another to come alongside him in his weakness. This provision of another is a blessing of God that must be proclaimed.

[49] John I. Durham, *Exodus*, Word Biblical Commentary, vol. 3 (Waco, TX: Word Books, 1987),

progression as the Lord's mercy deals with Moses."[50]

Whatever one's feeling about this theory, Durham succinctly states that Aaron served as a secondary leader to Moses and this so that Moses' reputation and leadership would not be compromised. Durham states, "Aaron is put in a relationship to him clearly similar to the relationship Moses has to Yahweh. . . . It is a remarkable struggle with the tension between the two figures, and one that leaves no doubt about Aaron's submission to Moses, just as the preceding paragraph leaves no doubt about Moses' submission to Yahweh."[51]

Aaron, being submissive to Moses, fulfilled Yahweh's plan by speaking authoritatively for Moses to the elders of the people and to Pharoah. The Scripture states, "Moses and Aaron brought together all the elders of the Israelites, and Aaron told them everything the LORD had said to Moses. He also performed the signs before the people, and they believed."[52] In this passage, Aaron acts as the spokesman for Moses and influences the Israelites to prepare to leave Egypt. When Moses and Aaron are to appear before Pharoah, the text reads, "You are to say everything I command you, and your brother Aaron is to tell Pharaoh to let the Israelites go out of his country."[53] Having been granted authority, he

---

50.

[50] J. A. Motyer, *The Message of Exodus: The Days of Our Pilgrimage*, The Bible Speaks Today, ed. J. A. Motyer, no. 3 (Downers Grove, IL: InterVarsity Press, 2005), 83. This author concurs with Motyer's rebuttal.

[51] Ibid., 50-1.

[52] Exod 4:29-31, *NIV*.

[53] Exod 7:2, *NIV*.

fulfills the role of spokesman as a subordinate leader and provides a great service for Israel and Moses as he ultimately speaks to Pharoah for God.

Through the mercy of God, Aaron is called into service to Moses. As will be seen in the chapter entitled Applied Theology, Aaron played a variety of roles to assist Moses. There is much that can be learned from Aaron's success in these roles and his failures when jealousy of Moses and pleasing people threatened his subordinate leadership.

Joshua's Subordination to Moses

Joshua Son of Nun had his name changed from Hoshea to Joshua by Moses.[54] He is first described by the Scripture as a leader of the Israelites, along with his 11 other companions who were to cross over the Jordan and explore the land of Canaan.[55] He and Caleb were the only two men from the 12 spies who went into the land to come back and say that Canaan could be overtaken by the Israelites. In a number of texts, Joshua is described as Moses' aide. Exodus 24:13 states, "Then Moses set out with Joshua his aide, and Moses went up on the mountain of God."[56] This formal designation of "aide" comes from the Hebrew verb *sharat*, meaning to minister or serve. The piel form of the word *shaw-rath'* occurs 96 in the Old Testament. Hermann Austel states, "Of the 96 occurrences, 20 are in the form of the participle . . . used as the noun 'minister.' . . . The use of *shaw-rath'* falls into two natural categories: (1) of the personal service rendered to an important personage,

---

[54] See Num 13:16.

[55] See Num 13:3.

[56] Exod 24:13, *NIV*; see also Ex 33:11, Num 11:28, Jos 1:1.

usually a ruler, and (2) of the ministry of worship on the part of those who stand in a special relationship to God, such as the priests."[57] The first use is that of the subordinate leader, denoting a special position as a servant, more than that of common menial employment, and was used of Joseph in Genesis 39:4, and Joshua in Exodus 24:13,[58] both men of substantial position.

This word is also used of Elisha as he ministered to Elijah in 1 Kings 19:21. It states, "Then he set out to follow Elijah and became his attendant (*shaw-rath')*."[59] This word is translated as "ministered unto him" in both the *KJV* and the *NASV*. The word is rendered "became his servant" in the *NKJV*, and is translated "became his attendant" in the *NIV*. Strong translates it as "to attend; contribute to; minister unto; do service unto; wait on."[60]

Other words that are translated as attendant or servant include *na'ar*[61] and *`ebed.*[62] The first term means boy, lad, servant, child, or youth,[63] and the second is translated slave,

<hr>

[57] R. Laird Harris, Gleason L. Archer, Jr., Bruce K. Waltke, ed., *Theological Wordbook of the Old Testament*, by Hermann J. Austel, (Chicago: The Moody Bible Institute, 1980), 958.

[58] Ibid.

[59] James Strong, *The New Strong's Complete Dictionary of Bible Words* (Nashville: Thomas Nelson Publishers, 1996), 548.

[60] Ibid.

[61] Ibid., Strong's #5288.

[62] Ibid., Strong's #5650.

[63] Ibid., 455.

servant, or subject, all denoting menial service.[64] Of *sharat*, Austel states:

> The high rank of the servant designated by this verb and the special relationship in which he stands in respect to his master is [*sic*] seen in Genesis 39:4. Here, Joseph was put over all the affairs of Potiphar's estate, and in vv. 8 and 9 Joseph was able to say that Potiphar did not concern himself with anything in the house. He left it all to Joseph's care, nothing being withheld from him except Potiphar's wife. In 2 Chronicles 22:8, King Ahaziah's nephews stand as ministers to Ahaziah. These men would obviously not be menials. In Esther 2:2 the king's attendants stand in a relationship close enough so that they have his ear and are able to make suggestions which the king follows.[65]

Clearly, Joshua is just one of many aides or attendants in a high position who served their lead leader effectively. The application of the various roles that he played will be made in the Applied Theology section below.

The Selection of Judges to Serve as Subordinate Leaders

Moses was a capable leader whose wisdom and counsel were sought day and night. Yet, his leadership was not complete. He had a tremendous burden that he alone was trying to manage and so he served each day as a judge presiding over the Israelites' disputes declaring what the will of God was for the various situations that they would bring to him. Upon seeing this, Jethro, Moses' father-in-law, offered Moses sage advice. He said, "What you are doing is not good. You and these people who come to you will only wear yourselves out. The work is too heavy for you; you cannot handle it alone."[66] This prescription to

---

[64] Ibid., 466.

[65] Harris, *Theological Wordbook of the Old Testament*, 958. The author must note that Joseph is not utilized in this theological foundation except here for illustrative purposes because of Bonem and Patterson's use of Joseph throughout their work, *Leading from the Second Chair*.

[66] Exod 18:17b-18, *NIV*.

employ additional capable leaders then followed. Jethro said:

> But select capable men from all the people—men who fear God, trustworthy men who
> hate dishonest gain—and appoint them as officials over thousands, hundreds, fifties and
> tens. Have them serve as judges for the people at all times, but have them bring every
> difficult case to you; the simple cases they can decide themselves. That will make your
> load lighter, because they will share it with you. If you do this and God so commands,
> you will be able to stand the strain, and all these people will go home satisfied.[67]

Moses took these steps as his father-in-law had instructed and established and empowered

subordinates to four different levels of leadership. He established judges to serve over

groups of thousands of people, then judges to serve over hundreds of people, judges to serve

over groups of fifties, and judges to serve over groups of tens. This simple plan of

empowerment provided a service to the people that he alone had been providing. In

establishing these various levels of leadership, he was able to delegate his responsibility and

authority to meet the needs of the people. In the Applied Theology section below the author

will examine the qualities and characteristics that these men were to possess that qualified

them to be judge. These qualities are vital today for subordinate leaders in the local church.

Subordinate Leaders from the New Testament

The Apostle Paul, like Moses, was a leader who had capable subordinate leaders

who served alongside him at various points of his ministry. Many of these helpers' names

were listed in his epistles. The apostle was known for his sending of these fellow workers

with authority to complete a task. H. Ritt states:

> For Paul the sending of fellow workers constitutes a mandate to carry out certain
> functions in the churches with authority. Thus Timothy is to strengthen the

---

[67] Exod 18:21-23, *NIV*.

Thessalonians in their lives of faith (1 Thess 3:2, 5), remind the Corinthians of the Pauline teachings (1 Cor 4:17), and inform Paul concerning the church at Philippi (Phil 2:19, 23; on Epaphroditus cf. Phil 2:25, 28). The primary tasks of those sent out (e.g., Tychicus: Col 4:8; Eph 6:22; Titus 3:12) are to take care of the collection (1 Cor 16:3; 2 Cor 9:3) and to gather news.[68]

Ritt's insight is helpful in seeing a few ways in which Paul made use of his second chair leaders, but his summation, as will be reflected below, that the primary task is to take care of the collection and/or gather news is inadequate. These tasks are overly simplified by Ritt to make his point, but as is seen below, Paul empowered these leaders in a variety of ways that ranged from preaching the gospel, to instruction in the way one is to live out their faith, to the establishment of officers for the local church.

Timothy, Subordinate Leader to Paul

Timothy is one of the clearest examples of subordinate leadership found in the New Testament. In him is found the complete picture of serving under the authority of another and being granted authority to lead and serve.

Timothy was known for being a disciple whose mother was a Jewish convert and whose father was Greek.[69] Paul wanted Timothy to join him on his journeys so he circumcised him and Timothy joined his ministry.[70] Timothy grew in his importance and service to Paul such that Paul included him in greetings to churches,[71] called him his

---

[68] Balz and Schneider, eds., *Exegetical Dictionary of the New Testament*, vol. 3, "Pempo," by H. Ritt, 68.

[69] Acts 16:1.

[70] Acts 16:2-3.

[71] Acts 20:4; Rom 16:21.

helper,[72] and sent him to the church of Corinth to instruct them and remind them about

Paul's way of life, demonstrating his being granted authority to lead.[73] In a later statement

in the same epistle, Paul says, "If Timothy comes, see to it that he has nothing to fear while

he is with you, for he is carrying on the work of the Lord, just as I am."[74] Clearly, Paul

views Timothy as a fellow worker in the gospel and as a critical leader in the movement of

the church. He is included in the salutation in 2 Corinthians 1:1 and is said to have preached

the gospel to the church in Corinth with Paul and Silas.[75] He is included in the salutation to

the church at Philippi, Colossae and Thessalonica, and is sent to Philippi and Thessalonica

as Paul's agent to encourage and strengthen these churches.[76]

Of their relationship, Paul calls Timothy his "true son,"[77] and says to the church at

Philippi, "But you know that Timothy has proved himself, because as a son with his father

he has served with me in the work of the gospel."[78] This term, "son," is not the usual Greek

term *uios* for son, but rather, *teknon*, for little child, "which emphasizes the relationship

involved, as over against *uios*, where the emphasis is more on the status of 'sonship'

---

[72] Acts 19:22.

[73] 1 Cor 4:17.

[74] 1 Cor 16:10, *NIV*.

[75] 2 Cor 1:19.

[76] Phil 2:19; 1 Thess 3:2.

[77] 1 Tim 1:2.

[78] Phil 2:22, *NIV*.

itself."[79] The term *teknon* is used 99 times in the New Testament in various forms and,

"refers to the child in relationship to its parents."[80]

Paul's second descriptive term concerning Timothy is *edouleusen*, which literally

means that he "performed the duties of a slave" in the work of the gospel.[81] Ironside states

of Paul and Timothy:

> As a son with a father, Timothy had commended himself to the aged apostle, serving
> with him in the gospel in all lowliness and humility. Youth is often exceedingly
> energetic, and impatient of restraint. Age is inclined, perhaps, to be over-cautious and
> slow in coming to conclusions, and it often is a great difficulty for two, so wide apart in
> years as Paul and Timothy, to labor together happily. But where the younger man
> manifests the spirit that was in Timothy, and the elder seeks only the glory of God and
> the blessing of His people, such fellowship in service becomes indeed blessed.[82]

Consider then Ironside's transition. "Having thus proven himself, Paul could trust

Timothy on a mission such as that upon which he was about to send him."[83] This delegation

of sending Timothy on this mission is a natural extension of trust that has been built between

leader and subordinate. This is what is to occur with lead leaders and subordinate leaders to

reach maximum effectiveness, as the lead leader grants authority to the subordinate leader.

One should take note of the descriptive phrases that Ironside used of Timothy in the

---

[79] Gordon D. Fee, *Paul's Letter to the Philippians*, The New International Commentary on the New Testament, ed. Ned B. Stonehouse, F. F. Bruce, Gordon D. Fee (Grand Rapids: Wm. B. Eerdmans Publishing, 1995), 268-9.

[80] Balz and Schneider, eds., *Exegetical Dictionary of the New Testament*, vol. 3, "Teknon," by Gerhard Schneider, 341.

[81] Fee, *Paul's Letter to the Philippians*, New International Commentary, 269.

[82] H. A. Ironside, *Notes on the Epistle to the Philippians* (Neptune, NJ: Loizeaux Brothers, 1976), 61.

[83] Ibid.

statement above. These phrases are "commended himself" and "lowliness and humility." These qualities mirror the example of Jesus. Jesus, too, served in lowliness and humility as He "did not consider equality with God something to be grasped, but made himself nothing, taking the very nature of a servant."[84]

Timothy models this picture of a subordinate servant as he served alongside Paul by serving with the interest of others at the forefront of his heart. There is much that can be learned from Timothy as a subordinate leader and this will be examined and further developed in the Applied Theology section below.

Titus, Subordinate Leader to Paul

Titus is another example of subordinate leadership in the New Testament. There is not as much information known about Titus as there is Timothy, but what is known is that he was a Gentile convert[85] who was a product of the ministry of the Apostle Paul.[86] Two texts in particular will give insight into the relationship between these two New Testament figures. The first is Titus 1:4, the second, 2 Corinthians 8:23.

In Titus 1:4 Paul utilizes the same term, *teknon*, to call Titus his true son that was used for Timothy. Albert Barnes notes, "This is language which the apostle would not have used of one who had been converted by the instrumentality of another."[87] This claim of

---

[84] Phil 2:6-7b, *NIV*.

[85] See Gal 2:3.

[86] See Titus 1:4.

[87] Albert Barnes, *Barnes' Notes on the New Testament*, ed. Ingram Cobbin, 11 vols. (Grand Rapids: Kregel Publications, 1976), 1186.

ownership can be translated, "My own son in the faith," or more correctly, "My true child in faith," giving a meaning of natural, or by birth relation.[88]

Titus was sent by Paul to the church of Corinth to complete the gathering of the offering that they had pledged the previous year for the poor believers in Jerusalem. The text states:

> So we urged Titus, since he had earlier made a beginning, to bring also to completion this act of grace on your part. . . . I thank God, who put into the heart of Titus the same concern I have for you. For Titus not only welcomed our appeal, but he is coming to you with much enthusiasm and on his own initiative. And we are sending along with him the brother who is praised by all the churches for his service to the gospel.[89]

Titus was also present with Paul for Paul's appearance before the elders and apostles in Jerusalem as they questioned Paul and Barnabas about the gospel they were preaching to the Gentiles. This questioning concerned the need for Gentile converts to Christianity to be circumcised according to the Law of Moses. On this occasion, Titus is thought by some scholars to be the example Paul used to demonstrate evidence of true conversion without a need for circumcision. The text from Galatians 2 states:

> Fourteen years later I went up again to Jerusalem, this time with Barnabas. I took Titus along also. I went in response to a revelation and set before them the gospel that I preach among the Gentiles. But I did this privately to those who seemed to be leaders for fear that I was running or had run my race in vain. Yet not even Titus, who was with me, was compelled to be circumcised, even though he was a Greek. This matter arose because some false brothers had infiltrated our ranks to spy on the freedom we have in Christ Jesus and to make us slaves. We did not give in to them for a moment,

---

[88] Marvin R. Vincent, *Vincent's Word Studies in the New Testament, Volume IV* (Peabody, MA: Hendrickson Publishers, n.g), 202.

[89] 2 Cor 8:6, 16-17, *NIV*.

so that the truth of the gospel might remain with you.[90]

Titus is also a key figure on the Island of Crete. On this island, Paul and Titus ministered together by preaching the gospel and establishing churches. This is the place and occasion for the pastoral epistle to Titus. In this letter Paul commissions Titus to appoint elders to these churches saying, "The reason I left you in Crete was that you might straighten out what was left unfinished and appoint elders in every town, as I directed you."[91]

One of the most compelling texts in helping one understand the relationship between Paul and Titus is found in 2 Corinthians 8:23. It states, "As for Titus, he is my partner and fellow worker among you."[92] The term for partner is *koinonos*, meaning companion or partner, an adjective of the term *koinonia*, and the commonly understood term for community, fellowship, or participation.[93] This use of *koinonos* is used twice by Paul, once in this text and again in Philemon 17. These uses indicate "A person with whom one is a partner or associate."[94] Further, the term carries a deeper meaning of obligation. J. Hainz states:

> As with *koinoneo* Paul uses *koinonia* also for various common relationships of Christians with each other. . . . This partnership is based on the mediation of the gospel by the apostle and in the common participation in the gospel and is expressed in common service for the gospel (or for Paul as its mediator). . . . A similar relationship in

---

[90] Gal 2:1-5, *NIV*; c.f. Acts 15.

[91] Titus 1:5, *NIV*.

[92] 2 Cor 8:23, *NIV*.

[93] Horst Balz and Gerhard Schneider, eds., *Exegetical Dictionary of the New Testament*, vol. 2, "Koinonia," by J. Hainz (Grand Rapids: Willam B. Eerdmans Publishing Company, 1991), 303.

[94] Ibid.

partnership exists between those who share together in the proclamation of the gospel. Thus Titus in 2 Cor 8:23 is described by Paul as "[with respect to proclamation of the gospel] my partner and with respect to you [the foundation and strengthening of the Church] [God's and] my 'co-worker.'"[95]

For Paul, Titus is naturally participating in the proclamation of the gospel because this is what one is to do as a recipient of the gospel message. Through their journeys together, Titus has become an example, an encourager,[96] and one empowered to go or stay on behalf of Paul, to accomplish the establishment of the church.

These two texts, Titus 1:4 and 2 Corinthians 8:23, give insight into Paul's understanding of his relationship to Titus. In summation, Paul has an expectation of partnership in the mission of establishing the church to the Gentiles from his true son in the faith. This partnership took place because Titus himself was eager to be a part of this redemptive mission of God. This is seen in 2 Corinthians 8 where Paul commends the Corinthian church to be prepared to receive Titus as he is sent on behalf of Paul and the other churches of Asia Minor. In this relationship one can see a mutual cooperation toward the establishment of the gospel and the strengthening of the church. From Paul, there is an expectation of cooperation and granting of authority to do the work of the ministry. From Titus, there seems to be a cooperation and eagerness to be utilized in whatever capacity needed to assist Paul in his God-given mission. This picture of mutual cooperation is critical for lead leaders and subordinate leaders of today's church and will be explored in the Applied Theology section below.

---

[95] Ibid., 304.

[96] See 2 Cor 7:6, 13.

Conclusion

As demonstrated above, the Scripture provides substantial material that demonstrates the formal relationship of lead leaders and subordinate leaders. Through an examination of the roles and relationships of the Trinity, leaders under Moses, and leaders under Paul, this author believes that there is an established theological foundation for subordinate leadership. This theological foundation can provide great insight for the subordinate leaders of today's church[97] and the application of this theological foundation for subordinate leaders in the local church will be developed and explored in the sections to follow.

---

[97] This author recognizes that he is stating a picture of the ideal when expressing the relationship of authority and subordination within the Trinity. Further, he recognizes that every first and second chair relationship will fall short of this ideal relationship.

APPLIED THEOLOGY FOR THE SECOND CHAIR

Given the establishment of lead leader/subordinate leader relationships in the theological foundation, this chapter will be devoted to demonstrating how the subordinate leaders mentioned above played significant roles in accomplishing the God-given task that was given to their lead leader. It is this author's belief that the expected outcomes of the theological foundation are various applications to the subordinate leader and lead leader of the local church. These applications are in the form of possible roles that subordinate leaders might play, insights into lead leader/subordinate leader relationships, and the discussion of character qualities that should be addressed in order for one to effectively lead from the subordinate leadership position. Prior to this examination, it is important to say a few words about authority structures in the local church.

A Brief Word on Authority in the Local Church

At this point, it is important to introduce some common practices of church governance. The author would like to establish that it is not his intention to seek to establish a specific ecclesiological model over and against another for the local church. Instead, regardless of the model of church governance, it is this author's intent to provide a resource that equips the subordinate leaders of local churches where it is understood that the subordinate staff members serve under the authority given to the senior pastor. Further, it is not this author's intent in this thesis to examine the degree of subordination on a ministry staff team or even a team of elders. Various churches utilize various models to govern the congregation that they are to serve. In many congregations there is a tremendous separation between the senior leader and the subordinate leaders on his or her team. This is a more traditional model. In other emerging congregations there is a small degree of separation that exists between the senior pastor and his or her subordinate staff members. As a matter of fact, it is this author's opinion that the terms subordinate leader and senior leader might be rejected by this group of leaders, as they elicit connotations of an old style of leadership that many of these progressive leaders have fled. Thus, instead of calling the first chair leader a senior pastor, there are title changes in the emergent church that call the first chair leader the lead pastor. Whatever the title, the principle is the same: there is ultimately a lead leader in almost every congregation. Gene Getz, in his work *Elders and Leaders* makes this statement: "The New Testament definitely teaches and illustrates that when there is a plurality of leadership, someone needs to function as the primary leader of the team."[98]

Though the single pastor, or as Grudem calls it, single elder[99] form of congregational leadership is the most prevalent in Baptist life, this author is not advocating or negating this particular model of congregational leadership. Many times the single pastor together along with the board of deacons will govern together and can by function become a plurality of elders.[100] Of these models, this author does recognize that they are both models

---

[98] Gene A. Getz, *Elders and Leaders: God's Plan for Leading the Church* (Chicago: Moody Publishers, 2003), 217.

[99] Wayne Grudem, *Systematic Theology: An Introduction to Biblical Doctrine* (Leicester and Grand Rapids: Inter-Varsity Press and Zondervan Publishing House, 1994), 928.

[100] Ibid., 930.

of authority and leadership that have been historically accepted by the church and that the

Scripture does not forbid these models of leadership in the local church. As for the

subordinate staff leader, many times this leader would not be considered to be in the group

of elders,[101] and at other times he or she would be.

In the common occurrence of the senior pastor/multiple pastoral staff model,

oftentimes the associate staff members report directly to the senior pastor and the senior

pastor works in conjunction with a group of elected deacons or elders. This is a very

common, accepted form of meeting the needs of a congregation. Like the model above, the

senior pastor and the elders or deacons would function as a plurality of elders, and most

associate staff members would not serve on these teams or possess the authority that comes

with the office of elder.[102]

Since most associate staff members will not occupy the office of elder, a number of

questions arise. First, from what source does the associate staff member derive his or her

authority? Second, does the counsel of Scripture give sufficient support for the role and

authority of the subordinate leader of the local church? Third, from the entire counsel of

Scripture, what are the best biblical examples for instructing the subordinate leaders of

---

[101] It is interesting to note that the role of the associate staff member is not addressed in Grudem's *Systematic Theology*. Grudem's approach is to address the different offices that have been given for the ruling of the church and he strongly advocates the "plurality of elders" approach. Yet, Grudem nowhere suggests that these elders might be other members of the vocational pastoral staff. Further, he seems to assume that if there is an elder that occupies another office in the church it is that of pastor/teacher. Thus, if there is to be a plurality of elders, then these are elected members of the church who work in conjunction with the senior pastor. As complete as Grudem's presentation is, it seems incomplete in dealing with the place for the associate staff member who has been called to serve the congregation in a specific role and who has been given authority to lead in this area of the church's ministry.

[102] This author does recognize that some models of church governance do include subordinate staff members serving in the role of elders.

today's church to assist them in how they are to properly serve the Lord Jesus and His church?

The answers to the first two questions are provided by the theological foundation but will be reviewed here briefly. In short, the subordinate leader of the local church is under the authority of the senior pastor of that local church. This can be seen in the ways in which the subordinate leaders mentioned in the theological foundation served their leader. In the Old Testament examples, Moses was commissioned by God and then provided additional leaders to assist him in his leadership journey. These leaders' subordination to Moses has been clearly established. In the New Testament examples, both Timothy and Titus are commissioned by Paul to accomplish the work that Paul the Apostle has been commissioned to do by the risen Christ. These men assisted alongside and served in a first chair/second chair leadership relationship. This too has been clearly established.

To the second question above, this author can confidently say, "Yes, the counsel of Scripture is replete with support for the role of the subordinate leader." As a matter of fact, this is God's design. It is the picture of authority and subordination that is modeled in the Godhead: as the source of all authority, the Father grants authority to those He is in perfect relationship with, and they, both Son and Spirit, are perfectly obedient to the will of the Father as they share in His redemptive mission. Oh, it is this author's desire that lead leaders and subordinate leaders in today's church might grasp this insight and work in such community and relationship that they reflect the image of the Godhead in the implementation of their ministry! This includes recognizing an equality of person, just as the persons of the Godhead are equal. Larry Kreider and his writing team state, "Along with the plurality of leadership, the New Testament teaches a co-equality within that plurality. Since every believer is on equal footing before God, and God does not show favoritism (Rom 2:11), no one elder should be exalted over another."[103] The authors, too, reference the relationships within the Trinity, and draw the distinction between equality as persons from that of responsibility. They state, "Although all elders are equal as persons, they are not co-equal in responsibility."[104]

The answer to the third question above "from the entire counsel of Scripture, what are the best biblical examples for instructing the subordinate leaders of today's church?" will provide the framework to the workshop designed to equip the subordinate leader of the local church. In the sections of this chapter that follow, the author will look at the various roles that the biblical subordinate leaders mentioned above played and how insight into these can assist both the lead leaders and subordinate leaders of the local church. Additionally, the author will examine aspects of these leaders' lives that the Scripture reveals to provide insight into the need for quality of character in the lives of subordinate leaders. This author does recognize that these roles are representative of a variety of roles that subordinate leaders play in their particular ministry contexts. Thus, these roles are not universal and absolute, but develop within the context of a ministry need.

---

[103] Larry Kreider et al., *The Biblical Role of Elders for Today's Church* (Ephrata, Pennsylvania: House to House Publications, 2004), 11.

[104] Ibid., 12.

Aaron's Service to Moses

Every leader has needs. Like every leader, Moses' leadership was not complete. To be frank, Moses had weaknesses as a leader. He had too many people to lead and to become effective as a leader, he had to learn to delegate and empower others to lead God's people as God directed him. As mentioned above, Moses was given Aaron as his first subordinate, and there is much that can be gleaned from the roles that Aaron played while serving Moses. Further, Aaron is also an example of caution and failure as a subordinate leader because of character issues.

Three Examples – Spokesman, Representative, and Wingman

The first role that was briefly discussed in the theological foundation is the role of spokesman. Because of Moses' inadequacies with his speech, God provided Aaron as a spokesman. Again, the Scripture states:

> Then the LORD's anger burned against Moses and he said, "What about your brother, Aaron the Levite? I know he can speak well. He is already on his way to meet you, and his heart will be glad when he sees you. You shall speak to him and put words in his mouth; I will help both of you speak and will teach you what to do. He will speak to the people for you, and it will be as if he were your mouth and as if you were God to him.[105]

As a result of this assigned role, Aaron was placed into a number of difficult situations as he served alongside Moses. The first was the need to persuade the elders of the Israelites that Moses and Aaron were there because of God's instruction to help deliver the people from Egyptian bondage. Exodus 4:29-31 states, "Moses and Aaron brought together all the elders of the Israelites, and Aaron told them everything the LORD had said to Moses.

---

[105] Exod 4:14-16, *NIV*.

He also performed the signs before the people, and they believed."[106] This role of

spokesman might not be a universal role for all second chair leaders, but in this instance, one

can see the principle of amplifying the vision at work in this subordinate leader. This was a

key role that Aaron played in helping motivate the Israelites to be prepared for and expectant

of a call to leave Egypt. As Aaron is preparing the people to leave Egypt, he is used to be a

spokesman about all that the Lord has done and he demonstrates the power of God to the

people by performing miraculous signs and wonders. The Scripture indicates the Israelites'

acceptance of this message from God and the people's willingness to follow Moses and

Aaron.

In a second episode of this particular role as spokesman, Aaron is the one speaking

to Pharoah for Moses. Exodus 7:1-2 states, "Then the LORD said to Moses, 'See, I have

made you like God to Pharaoh, and your brother Aaron will be your prophet. You are to say

everything I command you, and your brother Aaron is to tell Pharaoh to let the Israelites go

out of his country.'"[107] Roy Honeycutt states:

> The giving of Aaron as a spokesman in 6:28 seems clearly to parallel the earlier
> event in Exodus 4:14ff. . . . Earlier, the Lord indicated, "He [Aaron] shall be a mouth
> for you, and you shall be to him as God" (4:16). Within the present context the priestly
> narrator has stated the relationship in such a manner that Moses is not God to Aaron, but
> to Pharoah. . . . In the earlier source Moses is as God to Aaron (4:16); later this is
> ameliorated and Moses is God to Pharoah (v.1). The continuing significance of Moses
> is clarified, however, in the emphatic use of the pronoun: And you, you shall speak . . .

---

[106] Exod 4:29-31, *NIV*.

[107] Exod 7:1-2, *NIV*.

and Aaron your brother shall tell Pharoah (v. 2).[108]

In this Scripture the flow of authority that God has instituted of being the source of authority, granting authority, and providing others to walk in authority on behalf of another is in place. The important thing here is that Aaron is in the place of cooperation, submission, and usefulness to convey the message that God is passing on to Moses and he was willing to be placed in a difficult position as a spokesman to the King of Egypt for God's purpose.

Whether or not a subordinate leader in the local church will be a spokesman before a king is beside the point. What can be learned from Aaron as an example for other subordinate leaders is that he was willing to speak on behalf of another even in difficult circumstances to convey God's message. This role of spokesman can be intimidating and difficult especially when a subordinate is sent by another to convey a message but the subordinate does not have the background or full understanding of the situation.

Aaron also played the role of judge or representative. This occurs in Exodus 24:14 where Moses states to the elders of Israel, "Wait here for us until we come back to you. Aaron and Hur are with you, and anyone involved in a dispute can go to them." In the context of this story, Moses is taking Joshua, his aide, to the top of the mountain as Moses is going to meet with God. The Scripture indicates that Moses was gone for 40 days. During this period of time, Aaron and Hur are to fill the role of representative or judge on behalf of Moses. This author prefers the term representative because it demonstrates the temporary

---

[108] Honeycutt, Roy L. Jr, *The Broadman Bible Commentary*, ed. Clifton J. Allen, *General Articles Genesis – Exodus,* vol. 1 (Nashville: Broadman Press, 1969), 346.

vestment of authority to Aaron and Hur by Moses. This is more applicable to the local church setting over and against the role of judge. For example, periodically in the local church setting, the senior pastor might be away for an extended period of time, whether for ministry matters, family issues, or personal time away for renewal. In those times, the senior leader might look to his or her lead associate to fill the important role that they are leaving vacant.

In this text, Aaron and Hur are doing this for Moses. One might recall that Moses was the judge for the people and that he would sit all day and judge disputes.[109] Moses knew that this was a critical leadership role that must be carried on while he was gone, so he assigned two leaders to fill his role and temporarily vested this authority in them. Thus, the context of this specific role is not as substantial as is the leadership principle that Moses employed.

A third role that Aaron played for Moses is very much contextualized. As a matter of fact, this particular story will also be examined from Joshua's perspective in a later section of this work. This third role is a role that Aaron played along with Hur, and in this author's discussion with other subordinate leaders in the local church, it is a role that many identify with and look to for validation of their ministries. The role is what this author calls wingman. Exodus 17:8-13 states:

> The Amalekites came and attacked the Israelites at Rephidim. Moses said to Joshua, "Choose some of our men and go out to fight the Amalekites. Tomorrow I will stand on top of the hill with the staff of God in my hands." So Joshua fought the Amalekites as Moses had ordered, and Moses, Aaron and Hur went to the top of the hill.

---

[109] See Exod 18:13.

As long as Moses held up his hands, the Israelites were winning, but whenever he lowered his hands, the Amalekites were winning. When Moses' hands grew tired, they took a stone and put it under him and he sat on it. Aaron and Hur held his hands up—one on one side, one on the other—so that his hands remained steady till sunset. So Joshua overcame the Amalekite army with the sword.[110]

As Joshua takes a group of fighting men out to meet the Amalekites for battle, Moses takes Aaron and Hur to the top of a hill to see the battle from another plain. Keil and Delitzsch state, "Moses went to the top of the hill that he might see the battle from thence. He took Aaron and Hur with him, not as adjutants to convey his orders to Joshua and the army engaged, but to support him in his own part in connection with the conflict. This was to hold up his hand with the staff of God in it."[111] As Moses would hold up the staff of God towards heaven, Joshua and his men would be winning. Whenever his arms grew tired and the staff was not held up to heaven, the Amalekites would be winning. Aaron and Hur then come alongside Moses to see him through his physical burden of lifting the staff toward heaven. When Moses grew weary, these men placed him on a rock and came alongside him on either side and held his hands up so that the staff remained steady until sunset. Aaron and Hur each played the role of wingman, literally carrying Moses' burden with him to help lead the Israelites to victory over the Amalekites.

The subordinate leader of the local church can readily identify with this principle of carrying his or her leader's burden. This author has heard it expressed this way, "I feel called to be an Aaron or Hur, carrying my leader's burden for them as often as I can." Again, the story of Aaron and Hur as wingmen is contextualized to the hilltop as Joshua is in

---

[110] Exod17:8-13, *NIV*.

[111] Keil and Delitzsch, *Commentary on the Old Testament*, 79.

the valley of Rephidim fighting the Amalekites. Yet, the principle of service toward the lead leader should be universal. As stated above, every leader has substantial needs. This role of wingman, though not exclusive to men, is one of those substantial needs. A good wingman looks for ways to strengthen the first chair leader, especially in times where the first chair leader is heavily burdened by a challenging situation. A good wingman will come alongside his or her first chair leader and help lift and carry the burden for an extended period of time. To do this though, a subordinate must be a servant. He or she must have eyes that see past his or her own responsibilities, asking the question, "What does my leader need from me? What might he or she be burdened by and how can I assist him or her and lift this burden?"

This type of service is all too uncommon in the local church. This is demonstrated by the amount of attrition in subordinate staff roles on church staffs. This author is aware of the fact that high attrition rates on church staffs are not solely attributed to a lack of this type of service to a lead leader. Further, one might argue that the lead leader has a responsibility to pull the subordinate into situations and assign the task of serving in this way. Yet, much of this type of argument is based upon pride because a subordinate wants to be needed by his or her first chair leader. Often, without realizing it, a subordinate leader might wait to serve until they are called upon because they want the recognition for being asked to serve the lead leader in this way. What a subordinate leader must recognize is that he or she is in a relationship of service to the lead leader. He or she has been given responsibilities and authority to carry out his or her particular area of responsibility, but he or she is also in a unique position to lift the load and carry the burden of the first chair leader. The role of wingman is not going to be listed on a job description, but there is a clear application from the text listed above that at times a lead leader needs his or her burden lifted and God provides subordinate leaders to come alongside to lift this burden.

Rebellion in the Second Chair

Two other stories about Aaron's service to Moses are needed to help subordinate leaders understand the need for strength of character in a subordinate leadership position. The first story is that of Aaron's part in a rebellion by the Israelites while Moses and Joshua are on the mountain meeting with God, receiving the law. Exodus 32:1-6 states:

> When the people saw that Moses was so long in coming down from the mountain, they gathered around Aaron and said, "Come, make us gods who will go before us. As for this fellow Moses who brought us up out of Egypt, we don't know what has happened to him."
>
> Aaron answered them, "Take off the gold earrings that your wives, your sons and your daughters are wearing, and bring them to me." So all the people took off their earrings and brought them to Aaron. He took what they handed him and made it into an idol cast in the shape of a calf, fashioning it with a tool. Then they said, "These are your gods, O Israel, who brought you up out of Egypt."
>
> When Aaron saw this, he built an altar in front of the calf and announced, "Tomorrow there will be a festival to the LORD." So the next day the people rose early and sacrificed burnt offerings and presented fellowship offerings. Afterward they sat down to eat and drink and got up to indulge in revelry.[112]

It is interesting to note that at the appeal from the people, the Scripture gives no indication of hesitation on Aaron's part. Instead it appears he immediately responded to their requests to fashion a god out of gold. At their response of gifts of articles of gold, "He took what they handed him and made it into an idol cast in the shape of a calf, fashioning it with a tool."[113]

---

[112] Exod 32:1-6, *NIV*.

[113] Exod 32:4a, *NIV*.

To fashion something with a tool takes time, effort, and intentionality. It takes determination and a steadfast resolve. In this situation, Aaron takes time, and with his resolve, determination, and effort, intentionally fashions a golden calf for the people to worship, all the while knowing that Moses is on the mountain meeting with God. One must not read past this too quickly, but instead must consider all that Aaron has seen to this point from Yahweh. In light of all that Aaron has seen, his character flaw is fully exposed.

Consider for a moment that Aaron has seen Egypt suffer ten plagues sent by God upon Pharoah and his nation because of Pharoah's hard heart, and this all at Aaron's telling.[114] He has seen the Israelites plunder the Egyptians as they exited the country.[115] Aaron has seen God part the Red Sea so that the people of Israel might cross over on dry land, [116] and has visibly seen God lead them in the wilderness with a cloud by day and fire by night.[117] Further, every morning there was manna from heaven to sustain the people,[118] and Aaron, along with Moses, Nadab, and Abihu, and the 70 elders of Israel, went up on the mountain and saw the God of Israel. The text states, "Moses and Aaron, Nadab and Abihu, and the seventy elders of Israel went up and saw the God of Israel. Under his feet was something like a pavement made of sapphire, clear as the sky itself. But God did not raise

---

[114] Exod 9-11.

[115] Exod 12:35-36.

[116] Exod 14:21-22.

[117] Exod 13:21-22.

[118] Exod 16.

his hand against these leaders of the Israelites; they saw God, and they ate and drank."[119]

Yet, in spite of all of this, Aaron does not hesitate for a moment to erect a golden calf and satisfy the evil desires of the hearts of the people. One must ask whether or not Aaron wanted to be the lead leader of these people so much that he would give in to their wants and desires. This author recognizes that this is conjecture and that the text does not give insight into what he wanted, but his actions at least beg this question.

As the narrative continues, this author concludes that Aaron is the type of leader who wants to be accepted by everyone at all times. To this writer, he seems to be one who will say or do what others want to have said or done at that moment in time, and this he says or does because of a desire to be liked, needed, or accepted. This writer does not make this conclusion independently, but in light of Moses' and Aaron's exchange. The text states:

> (Moses) said to Aaron, "What did these people do to you, that you led them into such great sin?"

> "Do not be angry, my lord," Aaron answered. "You know how prone these people are to evil. They said to me, 'Make us gods who will go before us. As for this fellow Moses who brought us up out of Egypt, we don't know what has happened to him.' So I told them, 'Whoever has any gold jewelry, take it off.' Then they gave me the gold, and I threw it into the fire, and out came this calf!"[120]

From both Aaron's interaction with the people in the first part of Exodus 32 and here with Moses, it is evident that Aaron wants everyone to live at peace with him. His response to Moses, "Do not be angry, my lord," is indicative of his desire to be at peace with Moses. Yet, it is also clear that Aaron does not want to take responsibility for his actions. He

---

[119] Exod 24:9-11, *NIV*.

[120] Exod 32:21-24.

blames the people for being prone to evil and then states that he did give them what they

wanted, but the inference is that it is the people's fault because they are evil. Further, one

can clearly see Aaron's character flaw as noted above in his dishonesty with his brother

Moses. He states, "Then they gave me the gold, and I threw it into the fire, and out came

this calf!"[121] This lie is Aaron's attempt to escape his responsibility for evil action.

Previously, the text notes that Aaron "took what they handed him and made it into an idol

cast in the shape of a calf, fashioning it with a tool."[122] There is a tremendous discrepancy

between Aaron's account and what the text reveals previously. Again, Aaron intentionally

fashioned a calf out of the gold and he intentionally lied to Moses about how the calf

arrived. Durham states:

> The account of Moses' inquiry of Aaron concerning the calf can hardly be the
> attempt to exonerate Aaron it has sometimes been made out to be. . . . The answer of
> Aaron to Moses' attempt to find some excuse for his capitulation only makes Aaron's
> guilt worse by showing that he has no excuse, beyond expediency under pressure and
> his own weakness. . . . Aaron attempts to call attention away from his own involvement
> by putting the blame for what has happened on the people. He succeeds thereby only in
> appearing absurd: his accurate quotation of nearly the whole of what the people said to
> him (v 23 vis-à-vis v 32) loses its impact because he is not strong enough to let it speak
> for itself, and the lie about the calf emerging by itself from the fire is not a myth of
> divine autogeneration, but the dazzling insight of a master narrator designed to show the
> hopelessness of Aaron's leadership and perhaps the contrasting magnificence of the
> leadership of Moses.[123]

The story goes on to clearly blame Aaron for his failure in leadership as Moses'

representative while Moses was on Mount Sinai. It states, "Moses saw that the people were

---

[121] Exod 32:24, *NIV*.

[122] Exod 32:4a, *NIV*.

[123] Durham, *Word Biblical Commentary, Exodus*, 431.

running wild and that Aaron had let them get out of control and so become a laughingstock to their enemies."[124]

As an example to other subordinate leaders, it must be noted that Aaron failed Moses and God in the role he was given to act as Moses' representative. This failure occurred because of a character flaw in Aaron. Previously, while Moses is present with Aaron, Aaron's actions have been commendable and exceptional. Yet, to faithfully and adequately serve a first chair leader and the congregation the subordinate serves there must be a tremendous resolve of character to honor that leader's wishes when the leader is not present. This is especially the case in the extended absence of a leader. There must also be a resolve not to waver in the message being proclaimed by leadership to the people. If anyone wavered in the message being sent to the people, Aaron wavered. Previously, everything the people of Israel had experienced from Moses' and Aaron's leadership was the message of obedience to Yahweh. Yahweh was the one who had listened to their prayers, sent Moses, delivered Israel, and daily provided for their needs as they wandered through the desert. Yet, it appears here that Aaron is willing to disregard all that Yahweh has done if he can enjoy the allegiance of the people of Israel.

Though not abandoning Christ, like Aaron abandoned Yahweh, there are times the second chair leader in the local church can communicate something contrary to those in the congregation who might have a different agenda than the senior pastor. As a result, conflict arises, and often a subordinate leader can find themselves in the middle of a dispute or

---

[124] Exod 32:25, *NIV*.

power struggle for the direction a fellowship might go. When this occurs, the second chair leader must consider his or her allegiance and where it will rest.

It is this author's contention that a second chair leader must avoid sending a signal to the people that is contrary to what the senior pastor is sending; otherwise there will be consequences for everyone involved. There certainly were for Moses, Aaron, and the people of Israel. Moses had to desperately plead with God to forgive the sin of the people. His statement to the people about their rebellion is captured in Deuteronomy 9. It states:

> I fell down before the LORD, as at the first, forty days and nights; I neither ate bread nor drank water, because of all your sin which you had committed in doing what was evil in the sight of the LORD to provoke Him to anger. For I was afraid of the anger and hot displeasure with which the LORD was wrathful against you in order to destroy you, but the LORD listened to me that time also. The LORD was angry enough with Aaron to destroy him; so I also prayed for Aaron at the same time. I took your sinful thing, the calf which you had made, and burned it with fire and crushed it, grinding it very small until it was as fine as dust; and I threw its dust into the brook that came down from the mountain.[125]

Moses' intercession was costly and difficult. He fasted and prayed on behalf of the people and asked God to forgive them and withhold the wrath that everyone deserved. His statement about Aaron makes it clear at how displeased God was with him and how detestable his actions were, such that God might consider destroying him. Further, the way in which Moses dealt with the sinfulness of the people's revelry through empowering the Levites to kill those in rebellion also shows the consequences everyone incurred.[126]

---

[125] Deut 9:18-21, *NASV*.

[126] See Exod 32:27-29.

Jealousy in the Second Chair

One final picture of Aaron's failure lends to the body of knowledge available to second chair leaders. This is the occurrence of Aaron and Miriam's jealousy of Moses and their sin of speaking against Moses. It is interesting to note that the place of the offense is the tent of meeting, and the offenders take no pause to speak against Moses in the tent itself. The text states:

> Miriam and Aaron began to talk against Moses because of his Cushite wife, for he had married a Cushite. "Has the LORD spoken only through Moses?" they asked. "Hasn't he also spoken through us?" And the LORD heard this.[127]

What follows is both confrontation and judgment. First, God commands that Aaron and Miriam leave the tent of meeting. Then, he confronts their jealousy. In this, the LORD defends His servant Moses and the way that Moses humbly walks in obedience to the LORD. In essence, the LORD is drawing a distinction between the lead leader, Moses, and these two subordinate leaders, Aaron and Miriam. He states:

> "When a prophet of the LORD is among you, I reveal myself to him in visions, I speak to him in dreams. But this is not true of my servant Moses; he is faithful in all my house. With him I speak face to face, clearly and not in riddles; he sees the form of the LORD. Why then were you not afraid to speak against my servant Moses?"[128]

By this statement, the LORD is comparing their roles as priest and prophetess as secondary to the humility the leader possesses. Their question, "Hasn't he also spoken through us," gives indication of their elevated view of themselves and displays the pride in their hearts with which they ask this question. As a result of the pride of these spoken words, Miriam

---

[127] Num 12:1-2, *NIV*.

[128] Num 12:6b-8, *NIV*.

was made leprous, and both Aaron and Moses interceded for her.[129] Albert George Butzer

states:

> The words Miriam and Aaron spoke against Moses introduce a personal incident in
> which jealousy played a large part. . . . Miriam the sister of Moses was the chief
> offender. She herself was a prophetess envious of Moses' superior position. Observe
> how she endeavors to conceal her real motive of jealousy by the reference to the
> marriage of Moses. How characteristic that is of jealousy! But though we try to
> conceal it, soon we reveal it as did Miriam when she said, "Has the Lord indeed spoken
> only through Moses?" How often jealousy among religious leaders causes religion to
> suffer loss![130]

The application is clear: when leaders of the local church become jealous of one another,

the church will suffer, just like the people of God suffered when Miriam and Aaron became

Jealous of Moses.

A final word of application from the examination of Aaron for the subordinate

leader would be to walk humbly and speak carefully about the lead leader. No matter one's

view of the first chair leader, it is important to walk with Moses-like humility as a

subordinate leader, even when one is granted great responsibility and many are looking to

him or her for direction.

Joshua's Service to Moses

As seen in the theological foundation, Joshua son of Nun was Moses' aide. This

role was of tremendous importance to Moses. The Scripture says of Joshua that he was

---

[129] See Num 12:10-15.

[130] Albert Geroge Butzer, *The Interpreter's Bible: A Commentary in Twelve Volumes*, ed. George
A. Buttrick, *Volume 2* (New York: Abingdon Press, 1953), 200-01.

Moses aide from his youth, [131] and this term for Joshua is also the same term used for Elisha in his service to Elijah.[132] Like Aaron, Joshua played a number of key roles in his service to Moses. One role in particular will be discussed in the section that follows. Further, this author will then consider a few key characteristics of Joshua's character that will assist the subordinate leader in understanding the need for depth of character to be a successful subordinate leader in the local church.

The Second Chair as Warrior

In the narrative above where Aaron and Hur held up the arms of Moses on the top of the hill, Joshua's task was to select fighting men and proceed to the valley of Rephidim to fight the Amalekites. Exodus 17 states:

> The Amalekites came and attacked the Israelites at Rephidim. Moses said to Joshua, "Choose some of our men and go out to fight the Amalekites. Tomorrow I will stand on top of the hill with the staff of God in my hands." So Joshua fought the Amalekites as Moses had ordered, and Moses, Aaron and Hur went to the top of the hill. [133]

Many subordinate leaders in key second chair roles truly identify with Aaron and Hur standing alongside Moses on the top of the hill supporting their pastors by carrying their burdens. [134] Yet, few subordinate leaders continue to faithfully exegete the passage to see

---

[131] See Num 11:28.

[132] Though Elijah and Elisha were not thoroughly discussed in the theological foundation, this author will examine a certain process of development for subordinate leaders from the example of the relationship between Elijah and Elisha. This will come from the term *shaw-rath'* based upon the exegesis in the theological foundation pertaining to Joshua's relationship to Moses.

[133] Exod 17:8-10, *NIV*.

[134] www.secondchair.blogspot.com, Internet, accessed August 9, 2006. This quote was taken from www.secondchair.blogspot.com, the author's interactive weblog with other subordinate leaders across

that an additional subordinate leader was given the task to do battle for Moses and the

people. This role of warrior, though not popular, is one that subordinate leaders must take to

heart. John Durham states:

> Joshua is mentioned without elaboration as a military commander clearly subject to Moses' command. . . . Joshua is clearly understood in this narrative as the younger assistant of Moses and as the military leader he came to be (cf. Ex 32:17). . . . The abrupt introduction of Joshua in the passage at hand and in other passages as well may suggest that Joshua's early training as Moses' assistant was too well known to make details necessary.[135]

Thus, because of his subordination to Moses, and Moses' trust of him as his subordinate,

Joshua is given the responsibility to lead Israel's first battle in the wilderness.

For the reader of this thesis, the particular role of warrior that this author is

advocating is one that has come with personal experience and with what the writer would

describe as battle scars. This author believes that because he and his first chair leader have

had a strong, steady, lengthy, trust based, lead leader/subordinate leader relationship, he has

been able to serve in this way.

As the text denotes, Joshua was winning the battle with the Amalekites only when

Moses' staff was held toward the heavens.[136] Once the battle was won this is what the

---

the country. It states:

> That particular passage of scripture (Exod 17) is one that God spoke so clearly to us when our family came to this church. When we first heard the vision--which resonated with us . . . in the very depths of our spirits--we knew that God was bringing us here to be like Aaron and Hur and uphold the arms of our pastor. Given what we consider to be a mandate, whatever area(s) we have served in, our priority has always been to support him. We have been involved in ministry for years and have seen pastors struggling to do what they feel God has led them to do, and having no support in that vision or calling. And we've seen pastors fail . . . the hope that is in them shrivel up and die.

[135] John I. Durham, *Word Biblical Commentary, Exodus*, 235.

[136] See Exod 13:11.

LORD said to Moses:

> So Joshua overwhelmed Amalek and his people with the edge of the sword. Then the LORD said to Moses, "Write this in a book as a memorial and recite it to Joshua that I will utterly blot out the memory of Amalek from under heaven."[137]

It is interesting to note that the LORD would memorialize this event for Joshua. From the beginning of the account, Joshua was aware of Moses' ascent of the hill, but it is doubtful that he was aware of the activity taking place atop the hill.

This writer found comfort from the battle story of Exodus 17 because of two tasks he had to carry out as a subordinate leader in the local church. Both times, this writer had to "sling a sword" and could readily identify with Joshua, fighting a tough battle for the people of God. For Joshua, this call to lead a fight was clear because he could see the enemy attacking Israel. It was an easy choice to make to attack Amalek and his people because Joshua's people were threatened and under attack.

Unlike Joshua, this author's perspective was not as clear. Without getting into the details of the issues that were at hand, this author was given the responsibility on two separate occasions to ask church members to leave the church because of issues pertaining to their backgrounds involving sexual misconduct. This task was passed down from the senior pastor and a group of lay leaders who felt it in the best interest of the children of the church and the church as a whole to ask these two individuals to leave the fellowship. In hindsight, it has become clear for this writer that this action was the best action possible given the potential for harm to the children of the church. Yet, this author also was the one who

---

[137] Exod 17:13-14, *NASV*.

performed substantial ministry toward the individuals, first in an effort to redeem, and then additionally in an effort to keep tabs on them. As a result, this writer had the best relationship with them to convey the message from the collective leadership group that they were not to return to the fellowship.

As one can imagine, this was a very difficult task. For this author it felt as if he was driving a sword into the hearts of two individuals to whom he had been ministering, all the while not fully understanding the reasons why he was the one assigned to carry out this gross task. The only solace found was from the passage noted above. It has been this author's conclusion that to successfully navigate the challenges of the second chair, the subordinate leader must have faith and trust in the lead leader with which he or she serves. It was this passage where God instructed Moses to make a record of what happened on the hilltop that helped the writer understand this need for faith and trust in the lead leader. This passage provided this writer insight into the difference of being tasked by the leader to be a warrior and the burden the lead leader carries in seeing this role of judgment carried out.

In Exodus 17 there is an entirely different type of activity taking place on the hilltop than that which is taking place in the valley. This writer calls it the activity of the higher plain. Moses was instructed to inform Joshua of the activity on the higher plain that he might understand that he was not in the battle alone and that he did not grasp the entire picture of all that went into winning the battle against the Amalekites. Overwhelmingly, scholarship considers Moses' actions on the hilltop to be intercessory prayer to God for deliverance and victory. Keil and Delitzsch state, "The lifting up of the hands has been regarded almost with unvarying unanimity by Targumists, Rabbins, Fathers, Reformers, and nearly all the more modern commentators, as the sign or attitude of prayer."[138] This activity

of prayer and petition to God for Israel's victory comes from Moses' heart for his nation.

As a result of this message to Joshua, this writer has looked back on these two

difficult experiences with an appreciation of what was going on in the heart of the first chair

leader. Knowing his heart for God and his prayer-filled life, it was easy to reconcile that the

author did not fully understand all that was taking place on the higher plain between God

and the author's senior pastor. If assigned this role of warrior, a subordinate leader must

know that he or she might not fully understand the reason or rationale of the task at hand.

Yet, in obedience to the authority of the first chair leader and confidence in his or her

relationship with God, a second chair leader can faithfully execute the tasks at hand with

confidence that God is in control.

Joshua's Character as a Subordinate Leader

In contrast to Aaron, Joshua had strength of character that went against common

sentiment. On two separate occasions Joshua spoke up to make his opinion known to

Moses. The first is not well-known or terribly significant, but it demonstrates Joshua's zeal

and boldness as Moses' aide.

In Numbers 11 is found the account of Moses complaining to God about the task of

leading Israel while in the wilderness. In his complaining Moses asks God to put him to

death before he loses his honor and before all he has been doing for God is lost. He said, "If

this is how you are going to treat me, put me to death right now—if I have found favor in

---

[138] Keil and Delitzsch, *Commentary on the Old Testament*, 79.

your eyes—and do not let me face my own ruin."[139] At this complaint, God instructs Moses

to select 70 elders of Israel, "(men) who are known to you as leaders and officials among the

people."[140] These men were given to Moses to share the burden of leadership.[141] To signify

this event, the LORD shared the Spirit that rested upon Moses with these leaders and as a

result, they prophesied. Yet, a report from the camp came to Moses that two of these leaders

were not at the tent of meeting, but were instead in the camp. When the Spirit was placed

upon the group of elders, they too began to prophesy. At this report, one can see the passion

in Joshua for his leader Moses. The text states:

> Joshua son of Nun, who had been Moses' aide since youth, spoke up and said, "Moses, my lord, stop them!" But Moses replied, "Are you jealous for my sake? I wish that all the LORD's people were prophets and that the LORD would put his Spirit on them!" Then Moses and the elders of Israel returned to the camp.[142]

This response from Joshua shows a certain boldness and courage that he might assert

himself in this way. Though wrong in his assessment, Joshua was seeking to serve Moses in

a way to protect him from the confusion that might occur within the camp as the people

witnessed these men prophesying.

A good leader is going to allow his or her subordinates the opportunity to speak

into the various situations the lead leader might be facing. Sometimes this counsel might be

---

[139] Num 11:15, *NIV*.

[140] Num 11:16b, *NIV*.

[141] See Num 11:17. Though not the focus of this section of the thesis, it is interesting to note this process again of the granting of authority by one who is in authority that the burden of leadership might be shared by more than one individual. This instruction to Moses was initiated by the One who possesses ultimate authority and who in His divine plan has shared authority, both with the other members of the Godhead and with man, to accomplish His plan.

[142] Num 11:28-30, *NIV*.

correct and at other times incorrect. Whatever the case, a good first chair leader will see the opportunity to teach his or her subordinates from these situations. Like Joshua, a good second chair leader is going to feel comfortable expressing his or her opinion about various matters and confidently asserting him or herself into various ministry situations. This is a tremendous quality to have as a subordinate.

A second text that expresses Joshua's confidence in himself, Moses, and God's plan for Israel is the well-known story of the sending of spies into Canaan. After their investigation the spies returned to report on the land. Ten of the 12 spies were afraid and did not possess the confidence of Joshua and Caleb. The text states:

> Then Moses and Aaron fell facedown in front of the whole Israelite assembly gathered there. Joshua son of Nun and Caleb son of Jephunneh, who were among those who had explored the land, tore their clothes and said to the entire Israelite assembly, "The land we passed through and explored is exceedingly good. If the LORD is pleased with us, he will lead us into that land, a land flowing with milk and honey, and will give it to us. Only do not rebel against the LORD. And do not be afraid of the people of the land, because we will swallow them up. Their protection is gone, but the LORD is with us. Do not be afraid of them."[143]

Unfortunately, the people did not listen to the confidence and courage of Joshua and Caleb. Instead, they chose to listen to the ten other men who looked at the land and its inhabitants and were afraid. It is also interesting to now consider God's instruction to Joshua in the first chapter of the Old Testament book with his name on it. Joshua 1:6 states, "Be strong and courageous, because you will lead these people to inherit the land I swore to their forefathers to give them."[144] This command to be strong and courageous in light of the ways in which

---

[143] Num 14:5-9, *NIV*.

[144] Josh 1:6, *NIV*.

Joshua was a bold servant of Moses only seems to reinforce his character traits as a leader. In some ways, this is a message of affirmation and encouragement to Joshua from God to be strong and courageous as the lead leader just as he was as a subordinate leader.

One additional text to examine when considering Joshua's character while serving as a subordinate to Moses is Exodus 33:11 which states, "The LORD would speak to Moses face to face, as a man speaks with his friend. Then Moses would return to the camp, but his young aide Joshua son of Nun did not leave the tent."[145] This text, in the context of the rest of Exodus 33, denotes that this exercise was a common practice for Joshua. Verses 7 to 11 of Exodus 33 are inserted into this chapter to convey Moses' usual practice concerning the tent of meeting. The verses before and after this section speak to the situation before Moses and the Israelites as to whether or not the LORD would go with them into Canaan.

It appears to this author that Joshua would spend significant time with God at the tent of meeting. There are no further words, except that he would simply stay at the tent of meeting. Might this be the way in which Joshua was prepared to serve Moses and his people? It is not certain, and in some ways, by this author, this is pure speculation. But it appears that this time spent with God was what might strengthen Joshua as a leader and follower. If this was true of Joshua then it serves as a good example for subordinate leaders in the local church that they too should seek to spend significant time with God to strengthen them for their various leadership journeys.

---

[145] Exod 33:11, *NIV*.

The Character Qualities of Moses' Judges

As noted above in the theological foundation, Moses was overwhelmed with his leadership responsibilities on a daily basis because he judged all the disputes of the people every day. The Scripture states, "The next day Moses took his seat to serve as judge for the people, and they stood around him from morning till evening."[146] At seeing this, his father-in-law Jethro, gave Moses advice on how to improve everyone's experience. He instructed Moses to select men of character who could serve as judges of four levels of the population. The text reads, "But select capable men from all the people—men who fear God, trustworthy men who hate dishonest gain—and appoint them as officials over thousands, hundreds, fifties and tens."[147] Gene Getz states, "Moses took this advice, which enabled him to make sure the needs of the people were met and at the same time to maintain his own priorities—to represent them before God and 'to teach' them God's laws and decrees."[148] Moses implemented this leadership strategy and improved his and the people's experience. But the important things to consider for the subordinate leader in the local church are the character qualities of these judges that qualify them as capable men.

The first quality that qualified them to be subordinate leaders was that they were to be men who feared God. In this community, this was the most important quality that these men were to possess. If these men did not fear God, they would disrupt all that Moses had been doing as Israel's leader. Getz states, "Imagine what would have happened if Moses

---

[146] Exod 18:13, *NIV*.

[147] Exod 18:21, *NIV*.

[148] Gene Getz, *Elders and Leaders*, 230.

had appointed assistants who were not qualified—dishonest and self-serving men who would have taken advantage of the people. His problems would have been multiplied many times."[149] In examining the text further, Moses still had the responsibility to be Israel's teacher and instruct them in the laws of God. It states, "You must be the people's representative before God and bring their disputes to him. Teach them the decrees and laws, and show them the way to live and the duties they are to perform."[150] As Moses teaches the people and acts as their representative to God, he must have subordinate leaders beneath him who support what he has been teaching and enforcing as the judge. For this to happen, these men must fear the law of God that Moses has been utilizing to settle disputes. This quality is the basis from which the others flow.

This quality also is to permeate the lives of subordinate leaders in the local church. The local church has been commissioned by the Lord Jesus Christ to carry out his mission of redemption. For this to happen, the church's leaders must be men and women who walk reverently with God and who fear Him with a reverence that leads to holiness. In Philippians the Apostle Paul states, ". . . continue to work out your salvation with fear and trembling, for it is God who works in you to will and to act according to his good purpose."[151] For God to accomplish His good purpose for His church, the subordinate leaders of the church are to walk humbly and reverently before Him.

The second quality that these men were to exhibit was that of being trustworthy.

---

[149] Ibid., 230.

[150] Exod 18:19b-20, *NIV*.

[151] Phil 2:12b-13, *NIV*.

The term trustworthy means that these men were to be dependable. They were to be men who were considered capable of getting the tasks assigned by Moses completed.

This quality is critical for subordinate leaders in the local church if the church is to accomplish all that God intends for it. If a senior pastor does not have capable, dependable, subordinate leaders serving him or her, the church will be limited in its effectiveness. Consequently, the effectiveness of the senior pastor is in direct correlation to the dependability of his or her staff. Moses was able to implement the strategy outlined by Jethro and it worked for everyone involved. It would not have worked if the subordinate leaders that Moses enlisted were not dependable or trustworthy.

The third quality that these men were to possess is that they were to hate dishonest gain. In other words, these men were to be honest. If they were not honest, then the highest bidder would receive the judgment in their favor. If these leaders were placed in positions of leadership and yet they did not detest dishonesty, they would have abused their powers in such a way as to create chaos and conflict within the camp. This would have backfired on Moses and would hinder his credibility as the lead leader of Israel. All too often, the people were already considering rebelling against Moses' leadership. Had he placed men in positions of leadership where they could be bribed for personal gain, then the people would surely have revolted and God's purposes would have been thwarted.

This type of credibility is critical in the local church as well. When stories of financial impropriety surface in the church, it is devastating. If the people of the church cannot trust the leaders of the church to handle the gifts that the people bring, then the work of God suffers, slows, and comes to a halt. The senior pastor must ensure that his or her leaders who handle the financial affairs of the congregation are above reproach and that these individuals, like the judges Moses selected, should detest dishonest gain.

Additional Thoughts on *Shaw-rath'*: Servant, Aide, Attendant

This section is dedicated strictly to the development of future first chair leaders. Through this research process, this author has noted that both Joshua and Elisha were the special servants of two significant leaders over Israel. As noted above, the term distinguishing their service is the Hebrew term *shaw-rath'*. This special designation was given to these men as they served their respective leaders, and yet both of them ultimately succeeded their leaders as the lead leader for the task that God had assigned to their leaders.

For Joshua, there is no hint of succession of Moses as the lead leader of Israel until Moses is nearing his death.[152] On the contrary, Elisha is anointed the next prophet over Israel when he and Elijah meet for the very first time. Yet, it is interesting to note some of the commonalities of their succession stories. T. R. Hobbs states:

> A point of note in this chapter (2 Kings 2) is an overt reminder of the traditions connected with Moses and Joshua. The similarities are quite extensive between this narrative, the narrative of the crossing of the Reed Sea (Exod 14), and the narrative of the crossing of the Jordan (Josh 3). . . . The similarities extend beyond the use of common words. The relationship of Elijah to Elisha is like that of Moses to Joshua, and both successors are appointed in similar fashion (Num 27:18-23; 1 Kings 19:15-21).[153]

This section will suggest a particular application of leadership development for those who are called to be first chair leaders, yet are developing in a second chair role. In

---

[152] See Num 27:12-23.

[153] T. R. Hobbs, *2 Kings*, Word Biblical Commentary, ed. David A. Hubbard, Glenn W. Barker, vol. 13 (Waco, Texas: Word Books, 1985), 19.

doing so, this author will examine this idea of succession in the roles and relationships of Joshua to Moses and Elisha to Elijah to suggest a means to cultivate and develop lead leaders for the future.

Elisha's Service Toward and Succession of Elijah

The formal relationship between Elijah and Elisha is an intriguing one that can help subordinate leaders better understand what it is to serve under the authority of the first chair leader in order to take on a lead leader role in the future. To fully understand the relationship that Elijah and Elisha had, this author will start at the conclusion of their relationship from the biblical account and then look back at the dynamics of their relationship. The last picture of their time together is found in 2 Kings 2:1-2. It states:

> When the Lord was about to take Elijah up to heaven in a whirlwind, Elijah and Elisha were on their way from Gilgal. Elijah said to Elisha, "Stay here; the Lord has sent me to Bethel." But Elisha said, "As surely as the Lord lives and as you live, I will not leave you." So they went down to Bethel.[154]

This process was repeated three times and then Elijah asked his servant, "Tell me, what can I do for you before I am taken from you?"[155] Elisha's reply is quite telling of his respect, admiration, and desire to serve alongside Elijah. He states in reply, "Let me inherit a double portion of your spirit."[156]

At the culmination of this relationship, one can see how Elisha has taken seriously the call to succeed Elijah as the prophet of God. In this request, Elisha is asking, "for the

---

[154] 2 Kings 2:1-2, *NIV*.

[155] 2 Kings 2:9a, *NIV*.

[156] 2 Kings 2:9b, *NIV*.

status as rightful heir to the prophetic leader's role. The phrase indicates twice as much as any other heir, not double the amount Elijah had."[157] It is a beautiful conclusion to their first and second chair relationship.

Elisha's love, respect, and admiration, as stated above, are expressed in a willingness to serve Elijah. An important lesson that future lead leaders should learn is that while serving as a subordinate who will ultimately ascend to this level of leadership, to properly serve the Lord, one must properly sow into this relationship with the lead leader. What second chair leaders might also experience, as Elisha did, is reciprocation of service, as the prophet finally asked, ". . . what can I do for you before I am taken from you?"[158]

This idea of reciprocation of service to one another is evidence of a subordinate leader's successful service to a first chair leader. This service in return is a tremendous blessing to Elisha, as the cloak that was used to call Elisha into the role of prophet is the item that was left behind to indicate a granting of his request of a double portion of the prophet's spirit.

Yet, what can be learned about Elijah and Elisha's formal relationship before it culminates in 2 Kings 2? The first glimpse into this relationship is seen at the calling of Elisha in 1 Kings 19. First, God's call to Elijah is to anoint new kings and a new prophet. The text states:

The Lord said to him, "Go back the way you came, and go to the Desert of Damascus. When you get there, anoint Hazael king over Aram. Also, anoint Jehu son of Nimshi

---

[157] Hobbs, *2 Kings*, 21.

[158] 2 Kings 2:9a, *NIV*.

king over Israel, and anoint Elisha son of Shaphat from Abel Meholah to succeed you as prophet."[159]

Oftentimes this anointing of the king or prophet took place well in advance of the actual ascension to these roles. As one recalls, David was anointed king over Israel while Saul continued to serve for many years in the role as king.

In this instance, Elisha is anointed for a future office. In the meantime, God had a time planned for Elisha where he would follow Elijah and be his subordinate "attendant" that he might learn from the prophet in preparation for the ministry that God had for him. His calling to the office of prophet is recorded in 1 Kings 19:19-21. It states:

> So Elijah went from there and found Elisha son of Shaphat. He was plowing with twelve yoke of oxen, and he himself was driving the twelfth pair. Elijah went up to him and threw his cloak around him. Elisha then left his oxen and ran after Elijah. "Let me kiss my father and mother good-bye," he said, "and then I will come with you." "Go back," Elijah replied. "What have I done to you?" So Elisha left him and went back. He took his yoke of oxen and slaughtered them. He burned the plowing equipment to cook the meat and gave it to the people, and they ate. Then he set out to follow Elijah and became his attendant.[160]

This call of Elisha is expressed by Elijah in the throwing of his cloak around Elisha. This action indicated to Elisha that he was to come and follow the prophet and be anointed as the next prophet. It is very clear that Elisha understood that he was being called into service. This is seen as he requests to return to his parents, as he slaughters the oxen and bids farewell to all of the people, then returns to the prophet to follow and become his attendant.[161]

---

[159] 1 Kings 19:15-16, *NIV*.

[160] 1 Kings 19:19-21, *NIV*.

[161] See 1 Kings 19:15-21.

The key ingredients for Elisha's success, as expressed in verse 21, were a willingness to follow, serve, and attend to Elijah. This season of following is what God used to prepare Elisha for the ascension into leadership as the prophet of God and it is what God still uses today in some leader's lives to develop them for His purposes.

Naturally, when a young leader feels a call or anointing to lead there is often a desire to attain this calling of leadership rather quickly. For many young leaders who are in training for the ministry, there is a desire to be in the first chair role as the senior pastor of the local church immediately. Many of these young leaders have completely given themselves over to this in their pursuit of theological training, and upon their graduation, feel prepared and compelled to begin leading the church as the senior pastor. For some of these men and women this will be the path that they need to take. Yet, many of these young leaders can lose sight of an opportunity to learn by following and attending to a better, stronger, more experienced leader than themselves.

What the story of this relationship between Elijah and Elisha teaches is a dynamic learning environment where Elisha observes and attends to the prophet. In this experience, the attendant becomes well aware of the needs of the prophet and with a clear understanding of ultimately taking on this role himself, the attendant seeks to faithfully sow seeds of assistance into the ministry of the prophet.

Thus, subordinate attendants must understand that this takes time, patience, and trust. To receive this type of training, future first chair leaders who are serving as subordinate leaders must view this time with a steward's eye and a spirit of contentment. This takes time for a second chair leader to settle into, but finding this place of contentment and looking to their future by serving another is a place of great freedom.

One could speculate that Elisha had to choose to be content in this role as the prophet's attendant, if he was to faithfully serve God and honor his calling. One must note the circumstances that Elisha walked into. Clearly, it was understood that the King wanted to kill Elijah. This edict was declared just before Elisha went to work for Elijah. Further, Elisha had to understand his service to the prophet as a part of the greater calling to be God's mouthpiece. Bonem and Patterson label this "Now and Later Stewardship" for subordinate leaders. This principal of service recognizes that today is just as important as tomorrow, and it is in today that God is preparing his servants for what He has for them tomorrow. Thus, today, God's subordinate servant is stewarding both today and tomorrow, faithfully serving while faithfully preparing for a future role of lead leader.

The significance of this special position cannot go unnoticed if one is to effectively serve as a subordinate leader while developing to be a first chair leader. One of the most important ways that a subordinate leader can serve his or her church is through the relationship to the lead leader. In this service, subordinate leaders must understand the nature of being placed in a special position to the lead leader to assist this leader in the great work that God has called and empowered him or her to do. Often, this position is not looked upon with honor or prestige by the subordinate. Yet, this is a tremendous place to learn, prepare, develop, and grow so that one can be deployed to the role of lead leader.

To complete this section, it is crucial to examine a Scripture that provides commentary on Elisha's service to Elijah after Elijah has ascended to heaven. It is this author's opinion that this commentary provides the greatest insight into Elisha's service to

Elijah. The text is 2 Kings 3:11 which states:

> But Jehoshaphat asked, "Is there no prophet of the Lord here that we may inquire of the Lord through him?" An officer of the king of Israel answered, "Elisha son of Shaphat is here. He used to pour water on the hands of Elijah."[162]

It is interesting to see that another subordinate leader makes this comment about Elisha. His commentary is that Elisha is qualified to be the prophet of the Lord because of the way that he served the prophet of the Lord. In other words, this special, intentional role of being the prophet's aide or attendant is exactly what prepared him to be the next prophet for Israel. Further, the actions of this service are expressed in the statement, "He used to pour water on the hands of Elijah."[163]

How might the church change when its leaders begin to serve one another in this manner? Would there be any impact or noticeable difference? This author believes that the change would be significant. One of the most significant changes might be the way that the first and second chair relationships are lived out, especially with an eye to the future. If lead leaders grasp the potential for training future lead leaders by an intentional apprenticeship process like the one detailed above, then the lead leaders have a significant purpose accompanying the day to day delegation and operations of the ministry of the local church. If first chair leaders will consider this type of partnership and invest in the next generation of leaders in this manner, then there is always a new group of called, qualified, and trained leaders emerging to lead the local church. This approach provides a more defined teacher/pupil process and allows for tremendous levels of trust, grace, and communication.

---

[162] 2 Kings 3:11, *NIV*.

[163] Ibid.

The opportunity for both the first and second chair leader to model service to one another is tremendous, and should impact the rest of the team as well.

Joshua's Succession of Moses

As stated earlier, Joshua was not given the indication of succession of Moses like Elisha was at his calling. Instead, Joshua served alongside Moses, year after year, as he watched an entire generation of Israelites die off. From his generation, only he and Caleb would enter the promised land that they were to inherit. As Moses is nearing his death and is instructed to ascend a mountain in the Abarim range to look over into the promised land, Moses makes a request of the LORD. The text states:

> Moses said to the LORD, "May the LORD, the God of the spirits of all mankind, appoint a man over this community to go out and come in before them, one who will lead them out and bring them in, so the LORD's people will not be like sheep without a shepherd."
>
> So the LORD said to Moses, "Take Joshua son of Nun, a man in whom is the spirit, and lay your hand on him. Have him stand before Eleazar the priest and the entire assembly and commission him in their presence. Give him some of your authority so the whole Israelite community will obey him."[164]

Two insights from this exchange should impact the way that lead leaders view the development of their subordinates. First, Moses' heartfelt request was that as a shepherd of the people, Moses longed for his flock to be tended long after his departure. One might speculate that at a minimum he did not want his leadership to be in vain. Further, it appears that he certainly still believed the promise of God for this next generation to inherit the land, and he wanted to ensure that there was a plan for succession before his death. A second

---

[164] Num 27:15-20, *NIV*.

insight is from the last verse of this portion of Scripture in which Moses is to publicly

commission Joshua in front of the people. In this service, he was to give Joshua some of his

own authority so that the entire community would follow him. Again, the one in authority

is seen granting authority to one who is subordinate, with the result being the furthering of

the mission of God. Yet, all along, Moses had given authority to Joshua to lead the people.

Time and again he tasked Joshua for substantial roles and situations, and Joshua faithfully

displayed his stewardship of these various responsibilities. Thus, this final commissioning

was a formal statement of the passing on of the leadership of the community to Joshua.

Take a moment to consider the effect of this succession plan in light of the local

church. How might senior pastors change their course of leadership in light of the

succession plan above? Might they consider some sort of apprenticeship that ultimately

culminates in a succession plan at their retirement or departure to another congregation?

Much has been made in recent days about "Level 5 Leadership,"[165] a leadership term

employed by Jim Collins in his work, *Good to Great*. This level of leadership is the type of

leadership where the first chair leader looks beyond his or her tenure as the leader of the

company and prepares the company for the next generation of leadership that is to come.

Collins writes, "Level 5 leaders want to see the company even more successful in the next

generation, comfortable with the idea that most people won't even know that the roots of

that success trace back to their efforts."[166] As a result, Collins concludes that many of these

---

[165] Jim Collins, *Good to Great: Why Some Companies Make the Leap . . . and Others Don't*, (New York: Harper Business, 2001), 21-22.

[166] Ibid., 26.

companies, where the CEO prepared for his or her succession, went from being good companies to great companies because they had developed a plan and leader who could continue the mission of the company towards the future. This concept should be considered by first chair leaders in the local church in their attempt to continue the expansion of the kingdom of God beyond their tenure in leadership. This author recognizes that many of the key lay leaders must also cooperate if this is to be successful, and ample time for a transition must be given to the congregation as a whole.

How often is a church stifled and stalled by a lack of planning when the senior pastor retires or leaves to go to another congregation? In their book, *Elephant in the Boardroom*, Carolyn Weese and J. Russell Crabtree advocate that a good senior pastor should be speaking the "unspoken" about pastoral transition with his or her leadership team in order to keep the congregation moving forward if and when he or she retires or is called to another congregation. These authors state that an average transition period for a local church is approximately eighteen months. During this time, a church's growth often stops and membership declines because there is no leader trumpeting the call to follow. Frequently, they argue, churches that were once very strong, suffer because there is no transition plan in place and it then takes an additional eighteen months to recapture what was lost once a new pastor is on the field. Crabtree and Weese state:

> Today, one prevailing stream of thinking about leadership transitions tends to be *illness-based*. A pastoral departure is treated like a terminal diagnosis; just as no one plans for cancer, no one plans for a leadership transition either. Once the leader has moved, grief sets in. Organic change has taken place. A death has taken place. The congregation is wounded in all the ways an individual is wounded by a personal loss, and it responds in a similar pattern. Denial, anger, depression, guilt, bargaining, and finally acceptance are the stages of grief played out in the congregation as the members

experience loss. An entire body of literature has grown up around this illness-based approach to leadership transition.[167]

One might argue that because of the way many congregations elect or call their leaders that a succession plan is not practical. This may be true, and what this author is advocating concerning this type of transition may be unattainable. Yet, should not a good leader begin to address pastoral transition and at least have his or her leadership team develop a plan that looks beyond his or her tenure as the leader? Further, should not the lead leader intentionally look, if possible, to develop a subordinate leader in such a way that when his or her leadership tenure is complete, the local church already has a capable leader in place if it so chooses? This author advocates that if possible, he or she should.[168]

For this to happen there must be a tremendous openness between the subordinate leader and the lead leader where they mutually serve one another's interests. The first chair might consider a development plan over a course of years that steadily empowers and teaches the nature of leading from the first chair to the second chair leader. This author believes that if a senior pastor will commit to the idea of intentionally developing subordinate leaders to be prepared to be lead leaders throughout the course of ministry, then the local church as a whole will be strengthened because its future leaders are being intentionally trained to take the lead leader role.

---

[167] J. Russell Crabtree, Carolyn Weese, *The Elephant in the Boardroom: Speaking the Unspoken About Pastoral Transitions* (San Francisco: Jossey-Bass, 2004), 19.

[168] It is not this author's intent to develop in this thesis the detailed process for this level of training and development from the first chair leader to the second chair leader. It is simply this author's intent to identify this principle found in the Scripture noted above and advocate that some type of intentional process be developed for leaders in the local church.

Timothy and Titus, Subordinate Leaders of the Early Church

Both Timothy and Titus were willing servants to the task of proclaiming the gospel and establishing the early church alongside the Apostle Paul. These men were traveling companions at various times on Paul's missionary journeys, commissioned for special assignments, and were both praised for their service to the Lord and His church. Yet, these men were companions on apostolic mission, not staff members of the local church. Though subordinate leaders in the early church, the roles played by them then were vastly different than the roles played by subordinate leaders of the church today. As a result, as above, the author will seek to discern the leadership principles that can be extracted from their service to Paul. These principles are ones to consider applying in the local church context.

Timothy and Situational Leadership

Quite often when the Scriptures mention Timothy, they speak of him being sent by Paul into difficult situations to teach, strengthen, and remind these churches of the gospel that Paul proclaimed. These statements in 1 Thessalonians and 1 Corinthians summarize Timothy's service in this way: in 1 Thessalonians 3:2-3, "We sent Timothy, who is our brother and God's fellow worker in spreading the gospel of Christ, to strengthen and encourage you in your faith, so that no one would be unsettled by these trials;"[169] in 1 Corinthians 4:17, "For this reason I am sending to you Timothy, my son whom I love, who is faithful in the Lord. He will remind you of my way of life in Christ Jesus, which agrees

---

[169] 1 Thess 3:2-3, *NIV*.

with what I teach everywhere in every church."[170]

The principle to consider here is one pertaining to sending in light of situational

leadership. As a head coach finds himself in a certain situation on the field, he will often

call on a specialist to run a particular play to relieve the situation at hand. It is this author's

opinion that it is valuable for subordinate leaders to look upon Paul's use of Timothy in the

light of situational leadership and to understand why a first chair might call on a certain

subordinate leader to assist him or her in various difficult situations.

Consider Paul's use of Timothy in the following ways and the statements that Paul

makes to the churches about Timothy. Both passages above, 1 Thessalonians 3 and 1

Corinthians 4, provide context to help the reader understand the situation into which Paul

was sending Timothy. 1 Thessalonians 3 states, "For this reason, when I could stand it no

longer, I sent Timothy to find out about your faith. I was afraid that in some way the tempter

might have tempted you and our efforts might have been useless."[171] Given the report that

the Thessalonian church was enduring persecution, Paul felt compelled that he and Silas be

left in Athens so that Timothy could set off to get a report concerning this church. Further,

as stated above, Timothy was also sent into this church to encourage and strengthen them in

the midst of evil persecution.

In the letter to the Corinthian church, Paul is dealing with immorality and crisis in

the church, such that he sends Timothy to them with this message: "For this reason I am

---

[170] 1 Cor 4:17, *NIV*.

[171] 1 Thess 3:5, *NIV*.

sending to you Timothy, my son whom I love, who is faithful in the Lord. He will remind

you of my way of life in Christ Jesus, which agrees with what I teach everywhere in every

church."[172] In both letters to these respective churches Paul has other companions that he

can send. Yet, both times he sends Timothy as his fellow worker in the gospel.

In many ways, to continue the sports analogy, Timothy is Paul's most valuable

player. In light of this analogy, consider again Philippians 2:19-23:

> "I hope in the Lord Jesus to send Timothy to you soon, that I also may be cheered when
> I receive news about you. I have no one else like him, who takes a genuine interest in
> your welfare. For everyone looks out for his own interests, not those of Jesus Christ.
> But you know that Timothy has proved himself, because as a son with his father he has
> served with me in the work of the gospel. I hope, therefore, to send him as soon as I see
> how things go with me."[173]

Paul clearly exclaims, "I have no one else like him," indicating his tremendous admiration

and respect of Timothy and his trust in him as a servant in the gospel. In other words,

Timothy was the man for a variety of situations because he had so faithfully proven himself

in Paul's sight.

A subordinate on a team having a number of subordinates might consider if he or

she is often called upon to serve the first chair leader in certain difficult situations. If so, that

subordinate must consider how well he or she is handling these situations and whether or not

the lead leader continues to call upon them to perform these various tasks. If not, then that

subordinate might consider who on the team is being called upon in this way and then seek

to understand why the first chair leader is calling upon this person. In other words, it is

---

[172] 1 Cor 4:17, *NIV.*

[173] Phil 2:19-23, *NIV.*

important to ask what qualities this key second chair leader possesses that have given him or her influence with the first chair leader so that he or she is utilized in this manner.

As it pertains to this principle of situational leadership, the subordinate leader of the local church should understand that at certain times the lead leader will send in a subordinate leader to handle a difficult situation. The subordinate leader should also understand that many times the lead leader will choose a subordinate leader based upon certain conditions. As a steward, it is important to conclude that when in these difficult situations, the subordinate leader should seek to be a faithful steward and serve the first chair leader faithfully.

Titus and Leadership Development

Larry Kreider and his coauthors state, "Government in the early church was first through Christ, then the apostles, and then through elders, who led churches."[174] Titus was neither an apostle nor elder, but Titus was given the great responsibility by Paul to complete the work that Paul had begun on the island of Crete and to appoint elders in the churches on the island of Crete. Thus, Titus was an apostolic representative. Getz states, "When he (Paul) authorized Timothy and Titus to appoint elders/overseers and to hold them accountable, he delegated this authority to these apostolic representatives."[175] Titus 1:5 states, "The reason I left you in Crete was that you might straighten out what was left

---

[174] Larry Kreider, et al., *The Biblical Role of Elders*, 9.

[175] Gene Getz, *Elders and Leaders*, 228.

unfinished and appoint elders in every town, as I directed you."[176] As Paul continues his

letter, he then gives Titus the qualifications for these leaders. Further, as Titus is to

"straighten out what was left unfinished," he is given instructions on what to teach and how

to treat various groups of people in the churches on the island of Crete. Paul placed a

significant amount of trust in Titus for quality leadership in spite of Paul's absence and

commissioned him to put in place leaders who could carry on the work of the local church in

both Titus' and Paul's absence. It appears by Collins' assessment, Paul could be considered

a "Level 5 Leader."

Paul understood that if the work of ministry is to continue, leaders who will

continue the ministry must be enlisted and the proper instruction of those leaders must take

place. Often, this is something that Paul did himself, but it does not appear to be something

that he could do on Crete. As a result, he empowers one of his trusted subordinates to

develop the leaders needed for the church to continue on Crete.

In this particular Scripture, Titus is called to appoint elders who are to govern the

church. This is a rare opportunity for someone who is not a first chair leader. Yet, in light

of how subordinates can look to this principle, one must not necessarily apply the principle

to elders only, but instead increase the scope of finding and developing leaders for ministry.

This role is often played by subordinate leaders and is one of the most natural ways that a

subordinate leader functions. Depending on the need, most subordinates are already filling

roles and placing people into leadership positions. Often-times the leaders are enlisted by

---

[176] Titus 1:5, *NIV*.

the subordinate for that subordinate's area of ministry, such as teaching a Bible study class or working in the youth ministry.

At other times, a first chair leader may launch a new church-wide initiative and seek to put together a team of people from within the congregation. It is likely that a good first chair leader will allow his or her subordinates to provide input into who should assist in filling out the positions on the team. It is here that a strong subordinate leader will be able to provide tremendous support to the lead leader by providing insight into key leaders for the tasks ahead.

Subordinate leaders can also assist the ministry of the local church by finding and developing new people to serve in ministry positions. To do this, the subordinate leader must be aware of potential leaders, engage them to ascertain their interest in serving, and then train and deploy them into a ministry position. In implementing this principle, subordinate leaders can assist in the continuance of the ministry of the local church and extend the ministry as it develops more leaders.

BIBLIOGRAPHY

Balz, Horst and Gerhard Schneider, eds. *Exegetical Dictionary of the New Testament, Volume 1*, Apostello. by Jan-Adolf Buhner. Grand Rapids: William B. Eerdmans Publishing, 1990.

_____, eds *Exegetical Dictionary of the New Testament, Volume 2*, Koinonia. by J. Hainz. Grand Rapids: Willam B. Eerdmans Publishing Company, 1991.

_____, eds *Exegetical Dictionary of the New Testament, Volume 3*, Pempo. by Hubert Ritt. Grand Rapids: Willam B. Eerdmans Publishing Company, 1993.

_____, eds *Exegetical Dictionary of the New Testament, Volume 3*, Teknon. by Gerhard Schneider. Grand Rapids: Willam B. Eerdmans Publishing Company, 1993.

Barnes, Albert. *Barnes' Notes on the New Testament*. Edited by Ingram Cobbin. 11 vols. Grand Rapids: Kregel Publications, 1976.

Berkhof, Louis. *Systematic Theology*. Grand Rapids: Wm. B. Eerdman's, 1938, 97. Quoted in Charles C. Ryrie, *Basic Theology: A Popular Systematic Guide to Understanding Biblical Truth*. Colorado Springs: Victor Books, 1999, 54.

Bonem, Mike, and Roger Patterson. *Leading from the Second Chair: Serving Your Church, Fulfilling Your Role, and Realizing Your Dreams*. San Francisco: Jossey-Bass, 2005.

_____. "Three Paradoxes for Every Second Chair Leader." *Injoy's, The Pastor's Coach: Equipping the Leaders of Today's Church* 6, no. 16 (August): 2.

Butzer, Albert Geroge. *The Interpreter's Bible: A Commentary in Twelve Volumes*. Edited by George A. Buttrick. *Volume 2*. New York: Abingdon Press, 1953.

Cladis, George. *Leading the Team-Based Church: How Pastors and Church Staffs Can Grow Together into a Powerful Fellowship of Leaders*. San Francisco: Jossey-Bass, 1999.

Collins, Jim. *Good to Great: Why Some Companies Make the Leap . . . and Others Don't*. New York: Harper Business, 2001.

Crabtree, J. Russell, Carolyn Weese. *The Elephant in the Boardroom: Speaking the Unspoken About Pastoral Transitions*. San Francisco: Jossey-Bass, 2004.

Durham, John I. *Exodus*. Word Biblical Commentary, ed. David A. Hubbard, Glenn W. Barker, vol. 3. Waco, TX: Word Books, 1987.

Evans, William. *The Great Doctrines of the Bible*. Chicago: Moody Press, 1980.

Fagerstrom, Douglas L. *The Ministry Staff Member*. Grand Rapids: Zondervan, 2006.

Fee, Gordon D. *Paul's Letter to the Philippians*. The New International Commentary on the New Testament, ed. Ned B. Stonehouse, F. F. Bruce, Gordon D. Fee. Grand Rapids: Wm. B. Eerdmans Publishing, 1995.

Garrett, James Leo, Jr. *Systematic Theology: Biblical, Historical, and Evangelical*. Vol. 1. North Richland Hills: BIBAL Press, 2000.

Getz, Gene A. *Elders and Leaders: God's Plan for Leading the Church*. Chicago: Moody Publishers, 2003.

Grenz, Stanley J. *Rediscovering the Triune God: The Trinity in Contemporary Theology*. Minneapolis: Fortress Press, 2004.

Grudem, Wayne. *Systematic Theology: An Introduction to Biblical Doctrine*. Leicester: Inter-Varsity Press and Zondervan, 1994.

Harris, R. Laird, Gleason L. Archer, Jr., Bruce K. Waltke, ed. *Theological Wordbook of the Old Testament*, by Hermann J. Austel. Chicago: The Moody Bible Institute, 1980.

Hobbs, T. R. *2 Kings*. Word Biblical Commentary, ed. David A. Hubbard, Glenn W. Barker, vol. 13. Waco, Texas: Word Books, 1985.

Honeycutt, Roy L. Jr. *The Broadman Bible Commentary*. Edited by Clifton J. Allen. *General Articles Genesis - Exodus*. Nashville: Broadman Press, 1969.

Ironside, H. A. *Addresses on the Gospel of John*. Neptune, NJ: Loizeaux Brothers, Inc, 1942.

_____. *Notes on the Epistle to the Philippians*. Neptune, NJ: Loizeaux Brothers, 1976.

Keil, C. F. and F. Delitzsch. *The Pentateuch: Three Volumes in One*. In vol. 1 of *Commentary on the Old Testament*. Peabody, MA: Hendrickson Publishers, 1989.

Kreider, Larry, Ron Myer, Steve Prokopchak, and Brian Sauder. *The Biblical Role of Elders for Today's Church*. Ephrata, Pennsylvania: House to House Publications, 2004.

Lawson, Kevin. *How to Thrive in Associate Staff Ministry*. Herndon, VA: The Alban Institute, 2000.

Motyer, J. A. *The Message of Exodus: The Days of Our Pilgrimage*. The Bible Speaks

Today, ed. J. A. Motyer, no. 3. Downers Grove, IL: InterVarsity Press, 2005.

Panneberg, Wolfhart. *Theology and the Kingdom of God*. Ed. Richard John Neuhaus. Philadelphia: Westminster, 1969.

_____. *An Introduction to Systematic Theology*. Grand Rapids: Eerdmans, 1991.

Peters, Ted. *God as Trinity: Relationality and Temporality in Divine Life*. Louisville: Westminster John Knox, 1993.

Pink, Arthur W. *Gleanings in Exodus*. Chicago: Moody Press, 1977.

Powell, Samuel M. *The Trinity in German Thought*. Cambridge: Cambridge University Press, 2001.

Ryrie, Charles C. *Basic Theology: A Popular Systematic Guide to Understanding Biblical Truth*. Colorado Springs: Victor Books, 1999.

Sanders, J. Oswald. *Spiritual Leadership: Principles of Excellence for Every Believer*. Chicago: Moody Press, 1994.

Strong, James. *The New Strong's Complete Dictionary of Bible Words*. Nashville: Thomas Nelson Publishers, 1996.

Tillich, Paul. *A History of Christian Thought: From Its Judaic and Hellenistic Origins to Existentialism*. Ed. Carl Braaten. New York: Simon & Schuster, 1968.

Vincent, Marvin R. *Vincent's Word Studies in the New Testament: Volume IV*. Peabody, MA: Hendrickson Publishers, n.g.

Ware, Bruce A. *Father, Son, & Holy Spirit: Relationships, Roles, & Relevance*. Wheaton: Crossway Books, 2005.

Westcott, Brooke Foss. *The Gospel According to St. John: The Greek Text with Introduction and Notes*. ed. A. Westcott. Grand Rapids: Baker Book House, 1980.

Whale, J. S. *Christian Doctrine*. Cambridge: University Press, 1941.

Yount, William R. *The Disciplers' Handbook: From Transmitting Lessons to Transforming Lives in Sunday School, 9th ed*. Fort Worth, TX: by William R. Yount, 2006.

7025634R0

Made in the USA
Lexington, KY
12 October 2010